Lawrence and the Arab Revolt
An Illustrated Guide

Joseph Berton

ANDREA PRESS

Author: JOSEPH BERTON

Design and typesetting: ANDREA PRESS / DISEÑO ENTRE2

Published by:
ANDREA PRESS
C/ Talleres, 21 - Pol. Ind. de Alpedrete
28430 Alpedrete (Madrid) SPAIN
Tel.: 91 857 00 08 - Fax: 91 857 00 48
www.andrea-miniatures.com
andrea@andrea-miniatures.com

Printed in SPAIN:
Gráficas Díaz Tuduri, S.L. (Bilbao)

ISBN: 978-84-96658-35-6
DL: BI-2790-2011

Table of contents

Lawrence in Cairo, 1918. Photograph by Harry Chase

Lawrence on campaign, 1918.

Lawrence in London, 1919. Photograph by Harry Chase

-Introduction-

It started with the movie. My interest in Lawrence was sparked by seeing the film *Lawrence of Arabia* sometime in the sixties. All that colorful display of action, the camels, the exotic locations, and in a war story too, left me wanting to find out more about the real T. E. Lawrence.

This pursuit of Lawrence has been a wonderful journey with many fascinating side trips. I started by reading the easy to find Lawrence books from the local libraries. Just several biographies in, I realized that there were many sides to this life. Garnett's book of Lawrence's letters and the compilation of essays in T. E. *Lawrence by his Friends* became favorites. Soon I was chasing down harder to find titles, from distant English booksellers.

The visual images in the David Lean film made me most interested in actual photographs of the Arab Revolt. Getting to the Imperial War Museum for the first time, and going through their photographs was most rewarding. Seeing so many photos that had never been reproduced before, including shots of officers I only knew by name but had no idea what they looked like, was exciting. Here were photos of the every day soldier and Bedouin too, shots that never made it into the standard published biographies. The archival librarians were also helpful in letting me see the backs of these photographs, studying the written identifications on the photos, sometimes in Lawrence's own handwriting.

After college, my trips to England always revolved around a research trip to an archive or two. Eventually I received permission to view the Lawrence papers and photographs at the Bodleian Library. Arrangements were made so I could also photograph Lawrence's dagger and headdress at All Souls. Footnotes in biographies led me to seek out original documents and war diaries. The Public Record Office, now called the National Archives, became a favorite place to visit.

My own collection of books and items related to Lawrence and the Arab Revolt began to grow. It was always hard to find special objects and I wasn't ever spending big amounts money to be on any bookseller's short list.

However, all trips to London started with a visit to the famed bookshop, Maggs Brothers. They were very kind to me, letting me look and learn. Occasionally I would even buy a special book or letter, forcing myself to ration out what little money I had left for the rest of my trip. It didn't matter because I was often overjoyed by the new addition to the collection. I would take home a Lawrence letter, leading to more research on whom the letter was written to and why did Lawrence mention this or that in it, always leading to more research.

In one Lawrence letter I bought, he mentioned his favorite war books, which led to me reading Sassoon and Manning and Elliot Springs. My interest in medals opened up more research into the many men who played an active role in assisting the Arab Revolt. As is typical with Lawrence, other roads are always opening up with more paths to pursue, more knowledge to gain.

Highlights on this Lawrence journey include fascinating people I have met along the way. On a trip to England in 1989, I decided to call Rory Moore, a veteran of the Imperial Camel Corps who rode alongside Lawrence, taking part on the raid on Mudawara Station. Over the phone, I asked if I could come to Leeds and interview him about his First World War experiences. He was gruff on the phone but I proved my knowledge on some obscure point about the Camel Corps and he invited me over. Greeting me at his door with an offer of a drink, we had an outstanding afternoon. He had already written about his experiences with Lawrence but I was more interested in his day-to-day life as a sergeant in the Camel Corps. It was during that visit I learned about the daily line up for the spoonful of anti-malaria medicine. The officers never trusted the men to take the medicine on their own so they lined the soldiers up like a bunch of school kids for their daily dose. I asked Rory what they ate on campaign. He said it was mostly the regular army rations supplemented with local fare but he did have one favorite meal. He would take one tin of bully beef, put it with an onion and a cup of water into a waterproof mess tin, and hang it from his camel saddle pommel. After an hour, the gentle motion of the camel's movement and the heat on the tin would produce a quite lovely stew. Now those were some nuggets you just don't get in books.

Another remarkable person is Mena O'Connor. Mena ran a linen shop in Newport, Rhode Island for decades. When she finally decided to sell the shop, a friend of mine interviewed her. He asked about her name and whether or not she was named after the Mena House in Cairo. She said, that yes indeed she was named after Mena House, and that her father had served with Lawrence in Arabia. Mena's father was Bimbashi Garland. My friend said you really have to talk to Joe. That led to a long phone conversation, soon followed up with a visit to Rhode Island to meet her. Mena never really knew her father; he died when she was quite young. He did leave some scrapbooks and photos with her mother that Mena presented to the Imperial War Museum. I showed Mena the research I had done on Garland, including the photographs of him I had found. One of these photos she had never seen before. It's a shot of Garland taken in Arabia, smiling. It's been one of my favorite photographs and now it's one of hers. She remembered that her mother said her father had a good sense of humor and how often he would laugh. Now Mena had special proof of that in her hands.

Another person quite helpful on this journey was Edwards Metcalf. Known as Ned, he was in his late seventies when I met him. The grandson of Henry Huntington of Huntington Library fame, Ned started collecting Lawrence in the early 1930's. It seems he had an unlimited budget to work with and he chased down the really good items, including original Lawrence manuscripts. Until he passed away in 2001, he would help sponsor Lawrence conferences held at the Huntington Library or Pepperdine University. Renowned scholars, including Jeremy Wilson and John Mack, would come in for the weekend and make presentations. It was a terrific opportunity to listen, learn and question what was going on with Lawrence. If Mr. Metcalf liked you, or you proved your knowledge on the subject to him, he would open even more doors for you. Ned showed me some fantastic items he had bought over the years and even sold me some of his duplicate books. He never lost his enthusiasm for a new discovery. His encouragement for me to keep digging, keep researching and to write about what you find, to share your knowledge with others, was rewarding guidance. At the Huntington, his collection is revealing special Lawrence related facts and will for many years to come. Researchers will have more letters and documents to work with, and information to compile and share, a lasting legacy for Mr. Metcalf.

In T. E. *Lawrence by his Friends*, many people that knew Lawrence recounted their own impressions and what he personally meant to them. Lawrence was guarded in

Agal of T. E. *Lawrence*

his friendships but each of these people felt their own relationship with him was special in a very unique way. Lawrence explained that he only showed certain facets of his life to certain people. This important book showed many of these different and fascinating sides of Lawrence, his character and his varied interests. You will find that your own journey with Lawrence will open up more and more facets of his life. One interesting thing will lead to another.

This book's strength rests in the photographs. Many are published here for the first time, found in archives during rewarding visits. Some of these photos were found as recently as this last summer. Museums and archives are becoming more user friendly, with technology allowing us to view entire collections from home. It also seems every year more discoveries surface publicly, as family members realize that people are indeed very interested in what their grandfathers did during the war in far off Arabia.

I hope this book will serve as a helpful guide on your own journey in pursuit of T. E. Lawrence.

Joe Berton
Oak Park, Illinois

Zebun of T. E. Lawrence, likely the robe worn in some of the London photographs taken by Harry Chase, modified into a dressing gown.

Sarah Lawrence and her first four sons.
Left to right: Thomas Edward, born 1888, William George, born 1889,
Frank Helier, born 1893, and Montagu Robert, born 1885.
Photograph taken at Langley Lodge, Fawley, Southhampton, 1894-95.

-Youth-

Thomas Edward Lawrence was born on August 16, 1888. His father was Thomas Robert Chapman, an Anglo-Irish landowner of a large estate twenty miles from Dublin in County Westmeath. Lawrence's mother's name was Sarah. She had met Thomas Chapman while employed as the governess of his four daughters. Thomas and Sarah had fallen in love and had secretly set up household in Dublin when their affair was discovered. His wife refused to grant a divorce and Thomas left his substantial estate and family and eloped with Sarah. They adopted the name of Lawrence, the name used by Sarah while governess. She herself was illegitimate and there is some doubt to her actual name. They would lead a strong family life and stay together until the death of Thomas Chapman in 1919.

Five boys would be born to Thomas and Sarah. Montague Robert was born in 1885. T.E. (known to his family as Ned) was born in Tremadoc, North Wales in 1888. Next born was William in 1889, Frank followed in 1893, born on the Channel Islands, and the last, Arnold was born in 1900.

The family moved around frequently, spending time in Wales, Scotland, the Isle of Man, and to Dinard, in Brittany, where young Lawrence learned French. From there the family went to the New Forest where the children could enjoy great

Four of the Lawrence brothers: Thomas known as Ned, Frank, Montagu Robert known as Bob, and Will.

outdoor explorations and start learning with a governess. In 1896, with young Lawrence now eight years old, the family finally settled in Oxford, moving into a recently built three-story brick house on the North side of town, leading a respectable middle class life.

Thomas Chapman retained a fixed income and did not have to work for a living. He was able to spend a good portion of his time fostering his sons' interests. He was an avid bicyclist and encouraged his boys to ride, providing them with the best of 'made to order' bikes. He had a strong interest in photography and had a fine camera made for him and eventually had an expensive model with a wide assortment of lenses built for young T. E.. He allowed his sons the freedom to actively pursue their own interests. With Lawrence, this was a growing love of knights, Crusades, and the Middle Ages. Soon young Lawrence was making long bicycle trips out of Oxford to make brass rubbings and study castles. He was in contact with workers digging out

Letter of Recommendation from A. W. Cave, Head Master, City of Oxford High School.

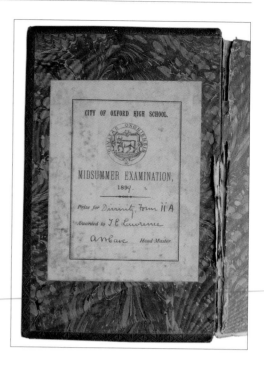

Cover and dedication page of a Prize Book presented to Lawrence by Oxford High School, 1899. Ismailia by Sir Samuel Baker, London, 1895.

new construction sites and urge them to save interesting archeological finds. Lawrence became a familiar face at the Ashmoleon Museum where he could study their medieval collection.

It was his mother Sarah though, that installed the discipline and insisted on a strict religious upbringing. The family attended church at St. Aldates where Canon Christopher offered an evangelical approach to Christianity and was more interested in saving the sinner, a message most comforting to Mrs. Lawrence. The Lawrence boys attended regular Sunday services and Bible study classes. Lawrence was a member of the Church Lads' Brigade and even briefly served as a Sunday School teacher. The family had additional daily family prayer sessions as well.

For their regular education, the boys attended the progressive City of Oxford High School for Boys. This newly opened grammar school already had a strong reputation and it had a good relationship with Oxford University. It was a small school, around 170 students, so the Lawrence boys were well known to the staff.

Lawrence himself excelled in some subjects and seemed above average in most others. He took honors in Divinity and in Greek and placed a joint runner up in a prized English essay contest.

While he did not care much for his formal education, he did find some teachers that were supportive and encouraging of his outside interests. He was a voracious reader concentrating on subjects like the history of the Middle Ages that interested him deeply. Athletically, he preferred to challenge himself physically with more individual pursuits like grueling bicycle rides and tended to avoid team sports

where size might play a role in one's success. Lawrence was just under 5'6" tall, but strong and very fit. He tested his body for long periods without food or sleep. His school friends remember him as being strong willed, independent, and with a good sense of humor.

It was during his teen years that his father had built for him a small bungalow in the Oxford house back yard. The parents recognized his need for independence and perhaps having separate but nearby quarters could lead to a more peaceful

The five Lawrence brothers: (left to right) T.E., Frank, Arnold, Bob and Will. 1910.

Jesus College, Oxford.

coexistence. His mother found him the must difficult of the boys. Lawrence soon decorated his quiet new quarters with brass rubbings. He stated to a biographer that when he was about ten, he also discovered the fact that his parents were not married. He was the only brother to have found this out and he never discussed this fact with his brothers while his father was still alive. He was certainly aware of the social consequences if the illegitimacy of the children became public. It did have an effect on how he viewed his mother and father and the weight of being illegitimate would bear on him for the rest of his life. Lawrence ran away to join up as a boy soldier with the Royal Garrison Artillery. His enlistment was short lived, perhaps just weeks. His father arranged to buy him out and brought him back home. It's an incident that Lawrence downplayed to his biographers. When it exactly happened is difficult to track down. The family denied the event but soon he was back in school preparing to take the exams needed for Oxford University. While some of his teachers did not see him as an intellectual, he did very well with his tests. In the Senior Locals he finished 13th in marks, with over 4500 students tested.

By October 1907, at the age on nineteen, Lawrence entered Jesus College, Oxford, and because of his Welsh birth, even qualified for a scholarship. He would study Modern History. He spent his first term living at Jesus College but then went back to stay at his bungalow in his parent's garden. Spending much time at home, making appearances at odd hours, occupying much of his time reading medieval poetry, sticking to a sparse diet, not using alcohol or tobacco, gave him an aloof and eccentric air. This did not stop him from making some close friends who would join him in rooftop climbing adventures and an occasional nighttime journey down an unknown underground waterway of Oxford. Even with this somewhat odd behavior, Lawrence joined the Oxford University Officers' Training Corps. He was an excellent shot and did remarkably well on the marches and outdoor endurance tests. In a preview of what lay ahead, a fellow officer candidate did point out that Lawrence never did seem to get his puttees wound correctly and "the hang of his uniform showed considerable eccentricity."

It was his interest in Crusades that would lead to summer excursions to research castles in Syria and France. This work would led to his thesis "The Influence of the Crusades on European Military Architecture – to the End of the XIIth Century." The summer of 1908 was spent doing an enduring bicycle journey through France. Keeping his family informed of his adventures, his letters home show a remarkable skill at observation. Armed with a camera and sketchbook, living mostly on cheese, fruit, bread and milk, he travelled over two thousand miles, making his way south through Montbard and Valence to the Mediterranean Sea and back north through Poitiers, Tours and Chartres to the channel. To continue his research, he had to prepare to travel to Syria and Palestine

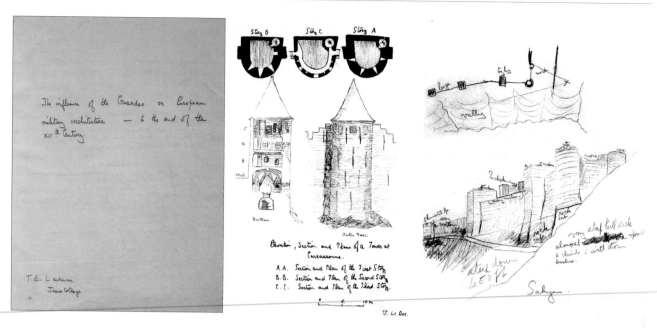

Cover page of Lawrence's B. A. honors thesis on Crusader Castles, gaining him a first-class degree in Modern History.

Lawrence's sketches and notes of a tower at Carcassonne, 1908.

Pencil sketch made by Lawrence at Sahyun.

Lawrence's pen and ink sketch of Sahyun made for his thesis, based on his on-site drawing and notes.

where he could observe and record the Crusader castles there. In preparation, Lawrence took simple Arabic lessons. D. G. Hogarth, Director of the Ashmoleon Museum and Lawrence's mentor gave him advice for his travels. Hogarth was a strong supporter of the budding medieval historian and would be influential for the rest

of his life. He encouraged Lawrence to meet Charles Doughty, the well-known Arabian traveler and author of *Travels in Arabia Deserta* and get his feelings on the project. Doughty strongly discouraged Lawrence to travel in the heat of the summer. It was a task that he would never encourage a friend to try, far too risky and hazardous

Postcard of High Street, Oxford with All Souls College in the background, circa 1910.

to one's health. Lawrence was not to be stopped. With a borrowed map, a proper camera, an automatic pistol and letters of introduction, Lawrence left to visit Crusader castles of the Middle East. By July 1909, he reached Beirut and set off for the castles south of the city. He almost immediately had a way of adapting to the country and its people. He would stay with locals at night or sleep in the open air. His letters home to his family document the people, places and adventures he would encounter. Lawrence shares a glimpse of his feelings with this letter to his father:

This is a glorious country for wandering in, for hospitality is something more than a name; setting aside the American and English missionaries who take care of me in the most fatherly (or motherly) way- there are the common people each one ready to receive one for a night & allow me to share in their meals: & without a thought of payment from a traveler on foot. It is so pleasant, for they have a very attractive kind of native dignity.

Though the walks were now more dangerous and difficult, Lawrence made his way to Aleppo and to the Homs, home to the huge Crusader castle Krac des

Chevaliers. He would spend three days photographing it and making drawings. When he resumed his travels, he wrote home:

I will have such difficulty in becoming English again, here I am Arab in habits and slipping in talking from English to French to Arabic unnoticing." Lawrence adds *"you will be happy now all my rough work is finished successfully; and my thesis is, I think assured.*

By the end of September, he had visited 37 out of 50 possible castles, had been mugged and robbed, suffered from malaria and was close to exhaustion. His walking journey covered eleven hundred miles. He wrote to the Principal of Jesus College explaining his delay in getting back to start the term, begging for forgiveness but relishing in *"a most delightful tour"* he had completed, living as an Arab with the Arabs. By mid October he was back in Oxford. Hogarth was greatly impressed by the fieldwork and first hand research completed by Lawrence in the most difficult conditions. Lawrence informed the legendary Doughty of his completed journey and how he hoped to return to Syria in little time. Over the next months he prepared his thesis for presentation. Examinations were held in June 1910 and with the strength of his thesis, Lawrence earned a first class degree in Modern History.

Lawrence's bungalow at 2 Polstead Road, Oxford.

Close up of Lawrence and Woolley, seated in front, with part of the Carchemish work force.
Dahoum is seated far right.

-Carchemish-

During the summer of 1910, fresh off of completing his studies at Jesus College, Lawrence obtained additional postgraduate research funds to study medieval pottery. His desire to return to the Middle East would be fulfilled when he was able to secure a field archaeologist position on a Hittite excavation at Carchemish. His mentor D. G. Hogarth was organizing the dig for the British Museum and though it was too late to get Lawrence a paid position, he did get him a scholarship through Magdalen College. Carchemish is located along the Euphrates River near the modern day border between Syria and Turkey. The next years would be the happiest in his life.

His journey just to get there was full of rewarding experiences too. Lawrence's travel benefited from being on a steamer that continually broke down leading to unplanned stops along the way. He spent an unexpected day in Naples and finally had a chance to experience the ancient city of Athens when the ship broke down once more. He long had a desire to see Greece, fueled by his readings of the *Odyssey*. He was not disappointed. He wrote home:

> I *walked through the doorway of the Parthenon, and on into the inner part of it, without remembering where or who I was. A heaviness in the air made my eyes swim, & wrapped up my senses: I only knew that I, a stranger was walking on the floor of the place I had most desired to see, the greatest temple of Athene.*

The steamer had additional mechanical difficulty, allowing Lawrence a layover in Constantinople for a week. On Christmas Eve, he arrived at Jebail, near Beirut, and he would stay there learning Arabic from a young Christian woman Farida el Akle, of the American Mission School. They would become close friends. By the end of February, Hogarth arrived in Beirut, met up with Lawrence and proceeded to Carchemish. The winter they were experiencing was one of the harshest and to make their way to Carchemish had to include sea and rail passage. Just getting there on foot or mule would be impossible. Part of this different route included riding on a section of the Hejaz Railway, this time being a passenger on the railroad

Entry to the Archaeologists' House, Carchemish.
The lintel, of Hittite design, was carved by Lawrence using a screwdriver and a knife. To the enjoyment of Lawrence, some visitors took it as an original Hittite carving.

that in a few short years he would be actively destroying. He and Hogarth even enjoyed dining at the station in Deraa.

By March, the party had arrived and was ready to start work. Carchemish was the site of an ancient Hittite city dating to 1500 BC. The British Museum had done some digging already but had stopped in 1881. Lawrence would inventory the finds, take photographs and help organize the work force of nearly two hundred hired local help. Lawrence demonstrated what could be a photographic memory in placing together collected bits of broken shards of pottery. Being the expedition photographer, he documented the latest archaeological finds but also shot wonderful portraits of his workers and the landscape surroundings. He did raise a level of official suspicion with his telephoto lenses since the dig location was close to a German bridge-building project, but he was certainly not a spy. It was a huge responsibility to hire and organize the work force. For a young man of twenty-two, he proved his ability to get along with the local population. He became aware of the local feuds and helped to mend them, studied the long-standing customs and shared in them. His workers found him to be a fair and unusual boss. He would sit down and talk to them, more as a friend than a supervisor.

One of the workers, Selim Ahmed, known as Dahoum, showed great promise. Lawrence got along well with the fifteen-year old, who wanted to learn English and advance his schooling. Lawrence taught him how to use the expedition's camera and Dahoum became his constant companion and assistant. It was a strong friendship that was misinterpreted by some of the Arab workers and Lawrence, in his own way of shocking the locals, did nothing to set the record straight. Some biographers have suggested a homosexual relationship, but Lawrence's friends and his brother denied it was anything of the sort. Though Lawrence was certainly tolerant of homosexual behavior, there is no evidence that he was an active participant. In his life, he would have some strong, intense friendships with women, but never dated or had any interest in marriage. While in Oxford he did become attracted to a young woman named Janet Laurie, though her own interest rested in Lawrence's younger brother Will. Laurie says that Lawrence actually proposed to her, though at the time, she just laughed it off. His own ideas of family were deeply affected by his knowledge of his illegitimacy, and he strongly wished his parents had never met. Lawrence did tolerate his married friends, even enjoyed some of their

wives' company and was godfather to a number of children. He would back away from people wanting to get too close, when not on his terms for what a friendship should bring.

Another Carchemish friend was the tough older fore-man Sheikh Hamoudi. He took care of Lawrence while he recovered from a severe bout of dysentery. The Turks ordered Hamoudi to not look after him. They didn't want an Englishman dying under their watch, but Hamoudi took responsibility and cared for him anyway. This local fore-man and Lawrence made quite a team to work for. Leonard Woolley, who became the supervising archaeologist writes they *"would suddenly turn the whole work into a game, the pick-men pitted against the basket-men or the entire gang against the wagon-boys, until with two hundred men running and yelling half a day's outlet would be accomplished in an hour; and Lawrence would lead the yells."*

There was no doubt that Lawrence was having an enjoyable time. He would be running around on some days in a Magdalen College rowing blazer and long shorts, bound at the waist by a brightly colored sash with long tassels. At other times he would be wearing native costume. He would later tell biographer Liddell Hart that these Carchemish years were the best years of his life.

During a break in the digs, Hogarth had arranged for Lawrence to work with the famed Egyptologist Flinders Petrie. Lawrence spent three weeks in Egypt digging out mummies in an ancient cemetery but found the work uninteresting and the job structure and expectations not to his liking. He was very satisfied when work resumed at Carchemish. This dig was quite productive with many carved reliefs and statues being

*Leonard Woolley and T. E. Lawrence at Carchemish, 1913. Woolley replaced Hogarth in 1912
and headed the excavations at Carchemish. Woolley recognized Lawrence's strengths, making him a valuable member of the team.*

discovered, each dutifully recorded and photographed by him. Lawrence also had time to explore the local territory, purchasing many Hittite seals for Hogarth and the Ashmolean. The more he travelled around the area, the more he came to realize the oppressive nature of the Turkish Government. The local Kurds spoke of freedom from the Turks. Lawrence was a sympathetic listener in their discussions of independence. There is evidence that he helped with getting weapons into the British base at Beirut when it was being threatened by a local uprising. Lawrence also offered information he was aware of regarding anticipated violence, to the American consulate. This was at a time when the Western governments would welcome information and observations from travelers or business people working in an area of interest. These people were not spies as such but their reports could be useful in building knowledge of local feeling. Lawrence also helped assist the victims of the cholera epidemic that was spreading around Carchemish. When smallpox broke out, Lawrence wrote for advice and supplies from his brother Bob, a medical student in London. Soon, he was helping the young children of the nearby village get vaccinated.

During the summer of 1913, when the dig was halted because of the hot weather, Lawrence went back to Oxford, bringing with him Hamoudi and Dahoum. The two Arab visitors had a remarkable time trying out various aspects of middle class English life. They amused the locals with their bicycle riding, while wearing their tribal robes through the streets of Oxford. They returned to Carchemish to finish what would be their final season.

During the digs, Lawrence had many visitors that would come by and see what the team was excavating. News had spread in the archeological circles of the outstanding work that was being done. A full-page article in the *Illustrated London News* informed the public of what was being unearthed. It sparked further interest and private donations to help with the excavation were brought in. The Arab traveler and writer Gertrude Bell came by and after some initial reservations about Lawrence, got on quite well with him and they developed a strong friendship with mutual respect lasting up to her death in 1926. She noted early on in one of her first observations that Lawrence would make a great traveler some day. Hubert Young, a young British officer in the Indian Army who would later serve with Lawrence in the Hejaz, passed through and saw firsthand how well Lawrence was managing the site and understanding the locals. Lawrence's brother Will came by on his way to a teaching position in India. Lawrence was so extremely pleased to have a family member come to Carchemish and see what he was working on. Will had been informed by the descriptive letters home that Lawrence sent but even he was surprised by the high regard the population held him. He was a lord of the place and absolutely enjoying himself. Will observed that he was most likely not going back to any calm desk job at Oxford. Lawrence himself said he could never trade this for a chair at the Bodleian Library. These Carchemish years were providing Lawrence with the perfect internship to learn skills and gain knowledge that he would rely on so strongly during his wartime service.

In December 1913, Lawrence and Woolley would be the archeological team called on to help with an extensive mapping of the Sinai area.

Living room of the Archaeologists' House showing a variety of rugs and artifacts collected by Lawrence and Woolley.

Cover of the Palestine Exploration Fund Annual volume containing
The Wilderness of Zin by C. Leonard Woolley and T. E. Lawrence,
dedicated to Captain S. F. Newcombe and published under the direction of D. G. Hogarth, 1915.

-Sinai and the Wilderness of Zin-

Lord Kitchener, victor of the reconquest of the Sudan in 1898 and now British Agent in Egypt, wanted a more complete survey of the Sinai Peninsula. He realized that this mostly unmapped territory would be crossed by Turkish troops, if they attacked the Suez Canal in the possibility of an upcoming war.

Because the Sinai was Ottoman territory, permission would have to be granted to the British by Turkey to proceed with its mapping. Turkey, though being courted by Germany to become an ally with Austria, was an uncommitted nation. The Turkish government did grant access. To give this survey party a legitimate decoy, the Palestine Exploration Fund got involved. Archeologists would record any traces of the Biblical exodus of Moses and his forty years of wandering in this wilderness, while the accompanying military engineers did the surveying work. The two archeologists offered the appointment, with the recommendation of Hogarth, were Leonard Woolley and T. E. Lawrence. As Lawrence noted to his mother, *"We are obviously only meant as red herrings, to give an archeological colour to a political job."*

Lawrence and Woolley, with Dahoum as servant, went to Beersheba, purchased local supplies and food. Royal Engineer Captain Stewart Newcombe, in command of the team, met the enthusiastic scholars and the six-week exploration was underway. He was expecting a couple of old diggers. From Newcombe, Lawrence would learn the importance of military mapping and geological observation. They got along well. This was his first time working with a professional soldier and Lawrence was an eager student. They would work together again soon, in the Hejaz during the revolt. While Newcombe focused on the mapping of the area, Woolley and Lawrence searched for remains of the biblical exodus but instead disappointedly found mostly Roman or Byzantine ruins. Of Kadesh, the burial place of Miriam, Lawrence writes that it *"is a filthy dirty little hole, and we more than sympathize with the disgust of the Children of Israel when they got there."* The Sinai was almost all rough terrain, inhospitable, with no local trace of Biblical remains. They did observe the passages through the mountains that the followers of Moses must have used. They were still travelled by the local Bedouin.

A side visit of the expedition was a trip to Akaba. Though a survey of the town already existed, this first hand observation of the small coastal town would aid Lawrence when he would

set the stage for attacking it just a few years later. He walked the same routes leading away from the sea, into the mountains that he would use in entering the town with Auda abu Tayi and the Howeitat, capturing it from the land. The local Turkish officials had grown suspicious of the party of archeologists and forced them to leave the area. From Akaba, Lawrence and Dahoum headed north to Petra. The site overwhelmed Lawrence. He wrote to his friend E. T. Leeds calling it the most wonderful place in the world, describing the rich colors of the rocks, urging him to see the place himself adding *"only be assured that till you have seen it you have not had a glimmering of an idea how beautiful a place can be."* Here, much to his surprise, Lawrence ran into two Englishwomen travelers. He used his charm to borrow money to help with his passage back to Damascus and eventually Carchemish.

By March 1914, both Lawrence and Woolley resumed their work at Carchemish. Hogarth had just raised funds to cover five more seasons of digging. However, local tensions were growing high when on the nearby German railway project a Circassian killed a Kurd leading to more violence. Lawrence and Woolley helped calm the situation, negotiating a peace. The Turks were so grateful they even offered the pair official thanks. When June came and the seasonal dig was finished, they both were to head back to England, but at Newcombe's suggestion, they took a longer route home, first to make observations of the German railway project underway in the Taurus Mountains. They were able to observe the progress, or lack of it, and report to the British military authorities.

On arrival in Oxford, Lawrence had to tackle the compilation of notes and photographs of the Sinai research and prepare it for publication. He also sought out different travelers' accounts that were previously published of the Sinai and incorporated them into his writing. Kitchener was anxious for the report to be finished, since the official work would only be completed with the actual publication of the archeological findings. Lawrence spent the summer putting the final work together. With the addition of Woolley's work, it would finally be published in 1915, by The Palestine Exploration Fund, with the title *The Wilderness of Zin*. Woolley and Lawrence are listed as co-authors. The initial urgency to publish was delayed when Europe plunged to war. On August 4, England declared war on Germany.

PLATE XXXIII.

(1) ROCK-CUT CISTERN IN WADY DEIRA.

(2) TYPICAL CHALK COUNTRY IN S. DESERT.

One of the 37 pages of photographs printed with nearly 150 pages of text.
The camel saddlebags, shown in the top photograph, contain surveying and photographic tripods and equipment.

PLATE XXXII.

(1) ROMAN BLOCKHOUSE BELOW NAGB EL SAFA (KURNUB–PETRA ROAD).

(2) NAGB EL SAFA.

The team documented mostly Roman and Byzantine ruins
in an often difficult and inhospitable terrain.

Postcard depicting Feisal and Hejaz flag, printed in Cairo late 1918.

-The Start of the War-

The Lawrence family would be affected greatly by the war. Bob, the oldest son, would finish his medical training and join the Royal Army Medical Corps in 1916. Will, teaching in India briefly served with the Ghurkas, but came back to England and was commissioned into the Ox and Bucks Light Infantry in April 1915. He would transfer to the Royal Flying Corps with 13th Squadron as an observer. Arriving in France, he was shot down and reported missing just a week later, near St. Quentin on October 23, 1915. Frank joined right away in August, caught up with the patriotic call to enlist and believing that the war would be over by Christmas. He was commissioned in the Gloucestershire Regiment. He was killed in action leading his men at Richebourg-l'Avoué on May 9, 1915.

It seems at the start of the war, Lawrence wanted to wait to see what opportunities would become available. He and Woolley were completing the *Wilderness of Zin*. Turkey was not yet in the war. Lawrence was hoping to land a job using his knowledge of the Middle East. Relying first on Newcombe, Lawrence eventually landed a position with Hogarth's help with the Geographical Section of the War Office in London. Though he started the work in civilian clothes, he was soon commissioned into the army as a 2nd Lieutenant on the "Special List," the category given to officers without a regimental affiliation. His talent was put to use right away working on a large-scale map of the Sinai and contributing to a Handbook of the area. By the end of October, Turkey joined the war on the side of Germany. Lawrence was already visualizing the Middle East without Ottoman control.

Lawrence readily accepted the offer to join the newly formed Military Intelligence Department in Cairo. It would be headed by Stewart Newcombe and together they left for Egypt on December 8, 1914. Leonard Woolley was going as well. Added to the staff was Aubrey Herbert, a Turkish expert and well-known linguist, and George Lloyd, an economic specialist with Turkish experience, both were Members of Parliament. Colonel Gilbert Clayton, a veteran of the Sudan campaign on 1898 and a trusted friend of Wingate and Kitchener, would be Director of Military Intelligence. Clayton had a wonderful leadership style that got the best work out of this group of cerebral and skilled unmilitary experts. Lawrence admired Clayton's willingness to listen as well. He was a loose director, not concerned about proper military tidiness and appearance. Lawrence said he *"made the perfect leader for such a band of wild men as we were. He was calm, detached, clear-sighted, of unconscious courage in assuming responsibility."*

The Intelligence Department had to interview prisoners, write secret reports, solicit agents, constantly update information and chase potential leads. Lawrence, because of his knowledge of Syrian dialects would interview many of the Arab nationalists. With his skill in maps and geography, he would work with the Survey of Egypt team updating their maps. Through long and tedious days, Lawrence was recognized for his efforts and tremendous contributions. Some officers found his casualness in dress and military rules unbearable but most people enjoyed his enthusiasm for the tasks at hand.

The deaths of his two brothers on the Western Front weighed heavily on him. Frank was killed in May 1915. On June 4th, Lawrence wrote to his father in a reassuring, support for your God and country way. *"I hope that when I die there will be nothing more to regret. The only thing I feel a little is, that there was no need surely to go into mourning for him? I cannot see any cause at all – in any case to die for one's country is a sort of privilege."* He urged his mother and father to put on a brave face, even suggesting it was their duty to do so. In October, Will was reported missing in action, after being shot down, and likely killed. Will was Lawrence's favorite brother and the tone of his feelings shifted dramatically. To his friend E. T. Leeds, on November 16th, Lawrence wrote:

First one and now another of my brothers has been killed. Of course, I've been away a lot from them, and so it doesn't come on one like a shock at all…but I rather dread Oxford and what it may be like if one comes back. Also they were both younger than I am, and it doesn't seem right, somehow, that I should go on living peacefully in Cairo.

In November, Lawrence was active in developing a new code for the British forces battling the Senussi in the Western Desert of Egypt. The Turks had cracked the old code and communications back to Headquarters was compromised. Lawrence himself delivered the new code to the Western Frontier Force at Sollum. When General John Maxwell wrote his official account of the Senussi war for the London Gazette, Lawrence would gain his first "mentioned in despatches" for performing exemplary service.

By March 1916, Lawrence was promoted Captain and would be asked to go on a special mission to Mesopotamia, with fellow intelligence officer Aubrey Herbert, a fluent speaker of Turkish. It was a most unusual assignment for just a Captain, but Lawrence was being recognized as one of the best intelligence officers in Egypt. Together with a Colonel Beach, they were to proceed deep into Mesopotamia, under a white flag to meet the Turkish commanders of the army. The Turkish army was close to forcing the surrender of General Townsend and his army, now in an exhausted state. The trio had orders to see if they could secure a safe passage of the army with an attempted bribe, up to one million pounds, for the Turkish command. Failing that, they would attempt to get the most favorable terms for surrender. The Turks realized they held the stronger hand and it would be only a matter of time before Townsend and his army would surrender anyway. Beach, Herbert,

General Sir Archibald Murray, Commander-in-Chief of the British forces, March 1916 to June 1917.

and Lawrence only achieved minor success by arranging an exchange of wounded soldiers for Turkish prisoners. Townsend surrendered before the British negotiating party

The Savoy Hotel, Cairo, headquarters of the British forces in Egypt and home of the Arab Bureau. Photograph by Harry Chase, 1918.

Sherif Hussein, Emir of Mecca, from the booklet The King of Hedjaz and Arab Independence, printed in London 1917, which included the entire Arabic proclamation of independence and an English translation of it.

was back to the British lines. Though Townsend and some of his staff were treated well, many of the British and Indian prisoners would fall ill or die during the march to Turkey.

Lawrence wrote a scathing attack on the situation in Mesopotamia, singling out what a messed up campaign it was. The report had to be toned down before it was sent on to General Murray, the Commander-in-Chief of British Forces in Egypt. Its stinging points were later supported by a Parliament investigation.

As an aside to the attempted bribery and negotiations, on this trip Lawrence was also able to meet with local tribal leaders and gather first hand information on the support of a native uprising against the Turks. There was only a luke-warm feeling for rebellion in this part of the Ottoman Empire. Lawrence and the British command realized their best hope now rested with Sherif Hussein of the Hejaz.

Sherif Hussein and the Start of the Arab Revolt

By the time Turkey declared war on the Allied powers, its empire was already showing signs of decline. The govern-ment had changed in 1908. Now run by the "Young Turks," the country suffered a series of defeats, first losing Bosnia-Herzegovina to Austria-Hungary, Libya to Italy and was soon forced to give up Macedonia. Germany was already heavily investing in Turkey by supervising the restructur-ing of its army, selling it weapons and training its officers. Though initially many of the Arab nationalists looked at this change of the Turkish government as a positive step, it soon became clear that the empowered "Young Turks" would deal with any unrest harshly. The former Ottoman Empire that displayed a certain tolerance for its many peoples and cultures was now strongly enforcing more re-strictive policies and increasing taxes. Secret underground societies of Arab nationalists were being formed. Their goal would be an independent Arab state.

Sherif Hussein held a strong political position amongst the Arabs. He was a descendent of the Prophet Mohammed and the designated 'Protector of the Two Holy Cities," Mecca and Medina. This was a hereditary title and before the war, his position was even strengthened by the Turks. He could see things were starting to change though. The Turks soon recognized his position as being potentially the leader of any nationalist movement. They began grooming his pro-Turkish replacement. By 1916, nationalist leaders were being executed in Damascus and Hussein's own sons' lives were being threatened. As early as April 1914, Sherif Hussein sent his second son Abdullah to Cairo for secret discussions with Lord Kitchener to get a feeling of British support for an Arab uprising against the Ottomans in the Hejaz. The British still held out hope that in any upcoming war, Turkey would join the British side or, at best, stay neutral. This changed when Turkey did enter the war in October 1914, siding with Ger-many. The British would again enter into discussions with Hussein about joining the Allied side. Written communica-

Emir Ali and Emir Abdulla at Abu Markha in Wadi Ais.

Emir Abdulla, 1917.

tion between the High Commissioner in Egypt Sir Henry Mc-Mahon and the Sherif Hussein began. Eventually, promises were made by the British government to support Arab national aspirations informing Hussein *"you may rest assured that Great Britain has no intention of concluding any peace in terms of which the freedom of the Arab people from German and Turkish domination does not form an essential condition."* The Sherif was still trying to get a deal out of Turkey, offering to join their war against the Allies if they would grant him Syrian independence. The Turks were not willing to go that far. Now Hussein decided to give his support to Britain, with the promise of Arab self-government.

Concurrent with these negotiations were the maneuverings of the French government to reestablish their stronghold in the Middle East. With historical connections dating back to Crusader times, the French wanted an active role in any post-war settlement regarding greater Syria and strengthening its colonial empire. Discussions between Sir Mark Sykes and Francois Georges-Picot led to a treaty in direct conflict with the agreements being made between McMahon and Hussein. It seemed that Whitehall had little awareness of what was being worked out in Cairo.

For strategic purposes, an Arab ally on the east side of Egypt would shore up the defense of the Suez Canal. It seemed reasonable for Britain to give up post-war colonial ambitions in

parts of the Middle East when the success of even achieving victory in this war was still in doubt. It would still be some time before the conflicting agreements would come to light and cause great anger, disappointment and broken dreams.

On early June, 1916 Sherif Hussein was ready to make his declaration of war against Turkey. From his balcony in Mecca, he symbolically fired a shot in the direction of the Turkish barracks and the war for Arab independence had begun. His four sons, Ali, Feisal, Abdullah and Zeid would each play important roles in the Revolt.

The Sherif Hussein commanded an unorganized, loose army of 6000 tribesmen and townspeople. With antiquated arms and no artillery, they were unable to capture the main barracks and Fort Jiad. Wingate understood the need to send help from Egypt. Soon four mountain guns and crew of the Egyptian Army arrived and a successful assault was made on the town. At Jidda, further British assistance from the gunships of the Royal Navy helped 4000 Harb tribesmen capture it. Further south of Mecca, Hussein's son Abdulla laid siege to Ta'if. The Turks would hold on at Ta'if for three more months, however, until heavier artillery arrived. Ali and Feisal, with a locally raised force of about 7000 men, had hoped to take Medina, but were met with stiff resistance. Fortified by a force of 11,000 soldiers with well-trained artillery, Medina would not surrender. Though the initial uprising had met with some success, the Turks were mounting counter attacks and forcing the Arabs to regroup. The Arabs were being hurt by their lack of modern guns, little ammunition, low supplies and no machine guns. The British command in Egypt had to determine how to aid the Arab Revolt, now that it was well under way.

Lawrence arrives in the Hejaz

After taking part in the disappointing mission to Mesopotamia, Lawrence returned to Cairo to resume his intelligence duties. There was a reorganization of the Military Intelligence Department that would affect Lawrence. Clayton had set up a new division, the Arab Bureau. Located in the Savoy Hotel, the most knowledgeable minds of the Arab Middle East would be brought together to form a strategy, compile intelligence, and develop a plan to assist with an Arab Revolt. Though not officially assigned to the Arab Bureau yet, Lawrence would help produce its written reports and even compile its first official newsletter of information titled the *Arab Bulletin*. He was proving himself extremely useful with his working knowledge of Arab affairs, the wide range of information he had gathered from his interviews with Arab informants and Turkish prisoners, and his continued enthusiasm for the Bureau's staff. Meanwhile, the relationships between Lawrence and his superior officers at the

Military Intelligence Department were becoming strained. By October 1916, Lawrence requested Clayton's help in arranging a transfer to the Arab Bureau.

By this time, the revolt started by Sherif Hussein in June was starting to lose momentum. The British were to send Ronald Storrs, officially the Oriental Secretary at the British Agency in Egypt, to Jidda to confer with Abdulla. Storrs would make first hand observations about the revolt, access its progress and determine how to help revive it. Lawrence, waiting for a decision on his request to transfer out of Intelligence and to the staff of the Arab Bureau, asked for leave to accompany Storrs. Lawrence already knew Storrs well, calling him the most brilliant Englishman in the Near East. They also shared likes in music and literature and just that summer worked together in designing the new stamps of the Hejaz.

The trip to Jidda would be Lawrence's first to the Hejaz. He too would also make observations of the revolt and of its leaders, reporting back to Clayton. His role officially was to act as an assistant. Clayton knew Storrs would handle the diplomacy well, but Lawrence would give him practical information. By October 16, Storrs, Colonel Wilson, the British Representative at Jidda, and Lawrence were meeting with Abdulla. Lawrence was not impressed by Abdulla at this initial conference, doubting his conviction to lead the revolt. In *Seven Pillars of Wisdom*, Lawrence writes, "*I became more and more sure that Abdulla was too balanced, too cool, too humorous to be a prophet; especially an armed prophet who, if history be true, succeeded in revolutions.*" After completing these formal discussions, Abdullah arranged for Lawrence to head north to meet his brothers Ali and Feisal, while Storrs returned to Egypt.

At Rabegh, the Hejaz coastal town on the Red Sea, Lawrence met Hussein's oldest son, Ali. He was 37 years old and Lawrence found him a "*very conscientious, pleasant gentleman, without force of character, nervous and rather tired.*" Ali arranged for Lawrence's travel to see his brother Feisal, providing him with two guides, a camel and Arab robes to cover his British uniform. Feisal was camped inland at Hamra in Wadi Safra, and they would pass through tribal areas that were not friendly to the cause. A difficult two day ride brought them to Feisal and his small army. It was in Feisal that Lawrence recognized the qualities he felt were needed for the leader of the Arab Revolt. Lawrence found him "*almost regal in appearance...far more imposing than any of his brothers.*" He adds in *Seven Pillars of Wisdom*, "*I felt at first glance that this was the man I had come to Arabia to seek – the leader who would bring the Arab Revolt to full glory.*" They had hours and hours of discussions. Part of one conversation Lawrence recounted, with Feisal asking him, "*And how do you like our place here in Wadi Safra?*" Lawrence answered, "*Well; but it is far from Damascus.*" Lawrence writes:

The word had fallen like a sword in their midst. There was a quiver. Then everybody present stiffened where he sat, and held his breath for a silent minute... Feisal at length lifted his eyes, smiling at me, and said, "Praise be to God, there are Turks nearer to us than that.

Lawrence would file his opinionated reports to Clayton and would realize what a challenging opportunity was now in front of him.

FEISAL'S ARMY ENTERING WEJH
Copyright

Photograph of Feisal's army entering Wejh, initialed by Lawrence from an annotated Graves biography.

Back to Cairo

Going to Yenbo, Lawrence put down his acute observations on Hussein's sons in writing and filed his reports to the Arab Bureau. He emphasized again that it was Feisal who showed the leadership qualities that would bring the revolt its best chance at success. He was sent with Storrs to make an opinion of the leadership available and Lawrence was quite clear with his own recommendation.

While getting the Royal Navy to provide him transport back to Egypt, Lawrence met Captain Boyle of the *Suva*. Boyle didn't think much of Lawrence on this first impression, with him wearing his Arab head cloth and carrying no baggage, hitching a ride. He was *'a little astonished when a small, untidily dressed and most unmilitary figure strolled up to me on board the ship I was temporarily commanding and said,*

hands in pocket and so without a salute; "I'm going over to Port Sudan." Their relationship and friendship would grow and strengthen during the revolt. Lawrence changed ships at Jidda where he met Admiral Wemyss on board the *Euryalus*. Wemyss and his willingness to help the Arab Revolt in any way were so critical in its eventual success. Now, he heard Lawrence's story. Wemyss asked Lawrence to accompany him to Khartoum where he would be introduced to Sir Reginald Wingate, the Commander-in-Chief of the Egyptian Army and formally Intelligence Officer for Kitchener during the reconquest of the Sudan in 1898. Wingate was now in charge of the military operations in the Hejaz. When they landed at Port Sudan to start their way overland to Khartoum, Lawrence crossed paths with Colonel Joyce and Captain Davenport, on their way to the Hejaz to take command of the Egyptian troops

Hejaz Regular Army soldiers and flag bearer.
This photograph appeared in French and British illustrated papers during the war, announcing the flag of the Hejaz.

there. Joyce, a career officer with the Connaught Rangers was a veteran of the Boer War and expeditions in the Sudan. He was taken back by Lawrence. In a post-war radio interview Joyce recalled his first impression. There was ' *an intense desire on my part to tell him to get his hair cut and that his uniform and dirty buttons badly needed the attention of his batman.'*

Lawrence made his way to Khartoum and shared his reports and impressions with Wingate. Lawrence stressed the immediate need for supplies and the want of British officers with knowledge of Arabic to serve as advisors to Feisal's army. Wingate had hoped for an Arab Revolt, was encouraged by what he heard, and promised to do what he could. Wingate also provided Lawrence four days rest in the governor's palace where he read one of his favorite books *Morte d'Arthur*.

When he returned to Cairo, Lawrence was officially transferred to the Arab Bureau. Detailed plans were being made on how to assist the Arabs at the coastal town of Rabegh. Colonel Bremond of the French Military Mission was pushing for a landing of Allied troops, mostly Algerian soldiers with French officers. Lawrence was strongly opposed to this plan of French intervention. He pushed an alternative plan on Clayton that would call for Arab tribes to defend themselves. What they really needed were more guns, ammunition, supplies, and advisors. He accused Bremond of having only his own motives in mind and leaving out any Arab interests. London debated the strategies. Soon Lawrence was called in before General Murray and he was asked to go back to the Hejaz. Initially Lawrence told Clayton he wasn't up for the job. He felt he was only suited for writing handbooks, editing the *Arab Bulletin* and drawing maps. With Clayton's encouragement, he was heading back to Yenbo, to be a military advisor to Feisal, a role he himself felt he was only half qualified to fill.

The Hejaz Flag

The new nation of the Hejaz needed a flag. Tradition has it that Hussein ibn Ali, the Grand Sherif of Mecca, designed the Hejaz flag, now known as the flag of the Great Arab Revolt. Originally, the first flags used by Hussein were a solid red, the color symbolizing the Sherif of the Hejaz and the Hashemites, who were descendants of the Prophet. The flag that become the symbol of the Arab Revolt incorporated stripes and a triangle in colors representing the great ages of the Arab empires. This design may have been collaboration between Hussein and Sir Mark Sykes of the Arab Bureau. In a letter to Wingate, Sykes sketched out several different plans for the Hejaz flag. It's most likely Hussein approved the final design.

The black horizontal stripe represents the Prophet Mohammad and the Abbasid Dynasty that ruled from Baghdad from 750 to 1258. During the rise of Islam in the seventh century, both white and black standards were used. The Abbasid Dynasty eventually adapted the black flag as a symbol of mourning for the assassinations of relatives of the Prophet and in remembrance of the battle of Karbala, where the army of the grandson of the Prophet, Hussein ibn Ali, was defeated, and he was killed.

The white horizontal stripe represents the Umayyad Dynasty that ruled from Damascus during 661 to 750. They chose white as their color of mourning and it is also used as a remembrance of the Prophet's first battle of Badr, a historic victory.

The green horizontal stripe represents the Fatimid Dynasty who ruled over North Africa and parts of the Middle East from 909 to 1171.

The red triangle at the hoist represents Hussein's family, the Hashemite, and the Sherifs, the descendents of the Prophet, that are the custodians if the Holy Cities.

The united symbolism of these colors was important to Hussein in designing this flag. He wanted to be the "King of

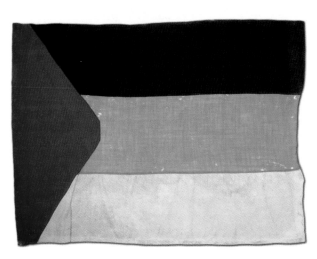

Hejaz flag presented to Brigadier General Macarthur-Onslow by Maulud el Mukhlus, famed Hejaz cavalry leader.

Hejaz flag stated to be from Feisal's Headquarters at Damascus. 24" x 37" with 1 ¾" gold fringe. Garst Museum, Greenville, Ohio. Donated by Lowell Thomas.

the Arabs." The British however, would only recognize him as the King of the Hejaz.

By 1917, the flag of the Arab Revolt was being carried by the Hejaz armies. Flags were also being distributed in liberated cities laying out in a symbolic way the Arab claims to the newly freed territory. By the time Damascus was captured, many flags were seen being waved out of windows and eventually hanging outside of the government buildings. As the British and Arab armies marched north to Aleppo and Beirut, Allenby was most aware of the political sensitivity of the Arab flag being displayed and ordered that no flag be flown in those areas.

Lawrence brought back a number of souvenirs from the war, including a Hejaz flag, and there are accounts of him running it up on a flagpole at All Souls College in Oxford.

The Arab Revolt flag was incorporated in the design of the Order of Al Nahda, given by King Hussein to British officers who provided valuable service to the Hejaz during the war. The award was presented in a silk-covered box, patterned like the flag.

Transjordan and Syria eventually adapted a modified Arab Revolt flag. The flag of Jordan has a white, seven-pointed star in the red triangle, and Iraq used a flag with two stars in the triangle. Today, many Arab nations and the Palestinian Liberation Organization use flags inspired by the Arab Revolt flag, with the same Pan Arab colors of red, black, white and green.

There are some surviving examples of this flag. The Imperial War Museum in London has a silk one on display. The Australian War Memorial has a flag in their collection given by Brigadier General Macarthur-Onslow, the commander of the 5 Light Horse Brigade in Palestine. He received it as a gift from, the commander of the Hejaz Regular Army. The Garst Museum in Greenville, Ohio has a silk flag donated by Lowell Thomas, identified as coming from Feisal's Head-quarters in Damascus. In 2005, Sotheby's auction house of London sold a flag of the Arab Revolt, owned by Captain Bedwell of the Royal Navy. He spent some time at Akaba at the end of 1918 and it is beleived he acquired the flag while there. This rare flag was purchased by the Kingdom of Jordan.

Auda abu Tayi and his cousin Mohammed el Dheilan with Feisal's standard bearer. Photograph by Harry Chase

Jordanian One Dinar bill depicting Hejaz troops with flag and the Order of Al Nahda with the modified Jordanian version of the Hejaz flag.

Um Lejj, a coastal city located between Wejh and Yenbo. 1917.

-Yenbo-

Lawrence arrived at Yenbo encouraged by the British response to the revolt and his endorsement of Feisal as its leader. Guns and supplies were starting to make thier way ashore to aid the poorly armed tribesmen. "Bimbashi" Garland, one of the first advisors to arrive, was training Arabs on the uses of explosives. Garland was a metallurgy expert sent to the Hejaz by Wingate. The Hejaz Railway, the single-track railway running from Damascus to Medina would be subject to their attacks. Lawrence was impressed by Garland's skills and took lessons from him as well.

Soon Lawrence headed away from Yenbo, back to Feisal's headquarters. Feisal welcomed him and took him on as an advisor. He asked Lawrence to wear Arab robes though, and to discard his uniform. By dressing as an Arab, it would give Lawrence more freedom around the camp; the tribesmen would know him as an advisor to Feisal. Lawrence had worn Arab clothing before while at Carchemish so he had no trouble in adapting to it. "It was a comfortable dress in which to live Arab fashion...Besides the tribesmen would then understand how to take me." He found

the robes much more suited for his tasks in the desert and gladly adopted them. He would rarely again don the British uniform during his stay in the desert. Colonel Joyce, his commanding officer in the Hejaz noted how the robes transformed Lawrence when he met him again in early 1917. Joyce recalls,

> On this occasion his appearance was such a contrast to the untidy lieutenant I'd met at Port Sudan, that one suddenly became aware of contact with a very unusual personality. He was beautifully robed in a black abbaya with a deep gold border, a kaftan of finest white Damascus silk with wide flowing sleeves, bound at the waist with a belt containing a large curved gold dagger; a keffiya or headcloth of rich embroidered silk, kept in place by an agal of whites and gold. Sandals on his bare feet. In every detail a truly picturesque figure indistinguishable from any of the nobles of the royal house of Hussein seated around us.

While most of the British officers and men in the Hejaz would wear the Arab headdress, few would wear the en-

Fakhri Pasha with Arab and Turkish officers at Medina. 1917-18.

tire outfit. Newcombe and Hornby did at times, but Garland complained about the impracticality of it, and how the corners of his head cloth would always blow up and smack the cigarette out of his mouth.

While with Feisal at his headquarters, Lawrence realized that the situation was changing fast. The Turkish army was on the move. Fakhri Pasha and his army headed out of Medina to attack the Arab tribesmen. His army quickly made advances west toward Yenbo with little resistance. Zeid, Feisal's younger brother, and his small army were easily defeated. It seemed Fakhri would push on and eventually recapture Yenbo. Garland was organizing a defense of the city with 1500 tribesmen, while Feisal's army would retreat there and be ready to help defend it. At Lawrence's request, the Royal Navy quickly arrived with five ships and saved the town. The Turks organizing for the assault saw the small fleet with naval guns ready and called off the attack. Lawrence felt that, by the Turks giving up the attack, it was right there that the Turks had lost the war.

Fakhri and his army moved south toward Rabegh. The troops of Ali and Zeid were being reinforced with help from the Royal Flying Corps. They had set up some planes and a landing field at Yenbo. Fakhri was also having trouble with his supply line. Getting materials sent all the way from Medina to his army was most difficult since they were subject to annoying raids from tribesmen. An additional Turkish column sent out from Medina was defeated and a large amount of gold seized. By mid January, Fakhri started to retreat back to Medina.

Lawrence wanted Feisal to move north, to take the coastal town of Wejh. Abdullah could maintain a protective position in the south, and move toward Yenbo or Rabegh, if needed. Feisal, by shifting his army northward, would apply more pressure by stretching out the Turkish troops needed to defend the Hejaz Railway. Feisal's army was on the move by the first week of January 1917. Over 8000 tribesmen took part. The Royal Navy provided needed help in the planned assault on Wejh. They would assist in landing an Arab force at the port, from the sea. At the same time, a land assault by Feisal's forces would attack by land. The plan was launched on January 23, without Feisal's forces, when three ships under Admiral Wemyss landed 600 Arabs. With support from the naval guns and some sailors taking part, the attack was pretty intense. By the next day, the Turkish commander ordered the town evacuated.

Feisal's army on the march to Wejh. January, 1917. Photographed by Lawrence.

Feisal and Lawrence however were having a difficult time making the journey to Wejh and keeping to the co-ordinated time schedule. The final stage of the march was made with little water or food. When they finally arrived the town was already in Arab hands and the garrison gone. Twenty Arabs from the attacking force had been killed and one pilot mortally wounded. Though Feisal and Lawrence were no-shows in the attack, it still went forward without them because there was fear that the Turks would retreat. Though pleased that the town had fallen, Lawrence was furious that the attack even took place. He felt these casualties were unnecessary and they simply could have been avoided. He was convinced that the surrounded garrison would have surrendered at no cost of life. It was not the first time Lawrence would butt heads with the professional officers over actions. However, Wejh was now under Arab control and would now be established as a base to make attacks on the nearby Hejaz Railway. With Abdullah and Ali staying in the south, Medina and its garrison would stay isolated, essentially trapped. From Wejh, the next move north would be Akaba.

Auda abu Tayi, standing center with Auda abu Zaal standing to his right and Auda's son Mohammed abu Tayi
with Zaal ibn Motlog on his left. This tinted photograph was taken in Amman in 1921 and sometimes credited to Lawrence.

-To Akaba-

After the capture of Yenbo, Lawrence was able to go to Cairo and take a week's leave. He wrote home filling in his parents with his latest adventures.

Things in Arabia are very pleasant, though the job I have is rather a responsible one, and sometimes it is a little heavy to see which way one ought to act...However it is very nice to be out of the office, with some field work in hand, and the position I have is such a queer one-...I act as a sort of advisor to Sherif Feisal, and we are on the best of terms, the job is a wide and pleasant one. I live with him in his tent, so our food and things (if you will continue to be keen on such rubbish!) is as good as the Hejaz can afford...

While in Cairo, Colonel Bremond met with Lawrence, on the pretense of congratulating him on the capture of Wejh. The talk soon shifted to Akaba. It was completely logical that if the revolt were to continue to shift north, the next coastal town to be taken was Akaba, two

hundred miles up the coast. Bremond was proposing his idea of landing an Anglo-French force there, from the sea. Lawrence told him that he knew the area well, from before the war, and that a sea landing would be too costly. Lawrence told him it would be best if Arab irregulars took Akaba, from the interior without Allied or naval help. Lawrence knew Bremond wanted French troops there to stifle the Arab movement and again he would oppose Bremond's plan.

When Lawrence returned to Wejh, he prepared Feisal for an upcoming visit with Bremond and to be aware of the push he would make for an Allied landing at Akaba. Feisal was raising more troops. He sent his 8000 man army back towards Medina and had recruited a new force of 8000 tribesmen. He also recruited in Egypt from among the many Syrian and Mesopotamian prisoners of war convincing them to join his forces. Some two thousand of these men would switch sides, now fighting for the Arab Revolt.

Tribes from the north were also coming to join too.

Said Ali Pasha and Egyptian officers at Wejh. Egyptian troops were used mostly in the Hejaz campaign in the south, working with Davenport and Garland. Later in the campaign, Peake commanded a group of Egyptian Camel Corps attached to Feisal's Northern Army.

Egyptian machine gunners near Jeida, east of Wejh.

Auda abu Tayi, the magnificent leader of the Howeitat, threw in his lot with Feisal. Lawrence recounts his appearance in Feisal's tent,

> I was about to take my leave when Suleiman, the guest-master, hurried in and whispered to Feisal, who turned to me with shining eyes, trying to be calm, and said 'Auda is here'. I shouted 'Auda abu Tayi', and at that moment the tent flap was drawn back and a deep voiced boomed salutations to our lord, the Commander of the Faithful: and there entered a tall strong figure with a haggard face, passionate and tragic. This was Auda and with him his young son, Mohammed, a child of eleven years old.

Lawrence had heard much about the warrior. "His generosity kept him always poor, despite the profits of a hundred raids. He had married twenty-eight times, had been wounded thirteen times, and in the battles he provoked had seen all his tribesmen hurt, and most of his relations slain. He himself had killed seventy-five men, all Arabs, by his own hand in battle, and had never killed a man except in battle. Of the number of dead Turks he could give no account: they did not enter his register." Auda wanted the revolt to move north to Akaba and was upset at the delay at Wejh. Feisal understood the political advantage of moving north, taking the revolt up into Palestine and Syria. For Lawrence, taking Akaba fit in with his strategic plan of irregular warfare, with an Arab army taking the town, and opening up a supply port linking it with the British army. He knew it would be a helpful link to Murray's plan for Sinai. Akaba was only 70 miles from the Hejaz Railway, easy striking distance for the Arabs.

Lawrence and Auda devised a plan to take Akaba from the landside. They would strike out northeast from Wejh, cross the railway, continue farther and swing back down again, southwest to Akaba. Lawrence notes, "This was the unguarded way, the line of least resistance, and the only possible one for us. It would be an extreme example of a turning movement, since it would involve us in a desert march of perhaps 600 miles to capture a trench within sight of our ships." On May 9, with Sherif Nasir as leader, Lawrence, Auda, Nesib el Bekri and a small force of Ageyl tribesmen left Wejh. They took with them twenty two thousand pounds in gold to entice the tribes to join them, fifty-nine pounds of flour per man, some spare rifles, and blasting gelatine for railway raids planned along the way. They would first head towards the springs of the Howeitat, two hundred miles distant. The journey became more difficult after several days of travel. Two camels were hurt and had to be destroyed. Lawrence became ill with fever and boils. They made their way to Wadi Jizil and crossed paths with Hornby, another British officer attached to the Hejaz, returning from a raid.

The landscape was turning incredibly harsh. Lawrence writes;

> *Nothing in the march was normal or reassuring. We felt we were in an ominous land, incapable of life, hostile even to the passing of life, except painfully along such sparse roads as time had laid across its face.*

They crossed flat burning lava flats leading to the Hejaz railway. They took some time to blow up sections of track and tear down telegraph poles. Resuming their journey they crossed over the landscape of El Houl, which offered no comfort. Lawrence noted that the "*Hejaz sun does not scorch but slowly blackens and*

consumes anything-men to stone-subject to it." To add further misery, sandstorms started to pound the men. To add to their discomfort, Auda feared possible raids by unfriendly tribesmen and had to set up guards in camp. Finally, they reached the well at Wadi Fejr with welcomed traces of green landscape. The meat of two gazelles was added to their diet of bread. They resumed by heading to the wells of Arfaja and across a corner of the Great Nefudh desert. Sandstorms continued and soon they were out of water once again. It was on the next day, May 24 that Lawrence noticed that one of his men, Gasim, was missing. Feeling he was personally responsible, Lawrence turned back and looked for him. After a two-hour search retracing their route, he found him, put him on his camel and started back to the group. Auda and two other men came back looking for Lawrence and helped with the final part of the journey. Auda was disgusted that Lawrence would risk his life for such worthless man. More harsh days of travel fol-

British Officers at Abu Markha at Wadi Ais. Left to right: Captain W. N. Montgomery R.A.M.C., Captain H. Garrod M.C., Captain H. Garland M.C., and Captain N. W. Clayton M.C. These officers worked primarily in the south with Abdulla's army.

NCOs of the Hejaz Regular Army. With the capture of Akaba, the British were able to land supplies on a regular basis. The Regular Army was formed with many liberated Arab troops from the Turkish Army. They were armed and uniformed with British equipment and tunics. The troops wear the longer Indian Army style kurta tunic.

lowed until they reached the well of Arfaja and by May 27, they reached the wells of the Howeitat. Soon tribesmen were coming in wanting to join Auda and his small army. Great feasts were held in the Bedouin tents with talk of marching straight on to Damascus. This strategy was discouraged. They had to stay on target with the taking of Akaba.

Lawrence was being torn by the British promises being made to the Arabs, and the treaties made between the British and French governments. Lawrence felt he was convincing the Arabs to fight and die on a lie. He realized the agreements were in conflict and felt the only way possible to realize Arab independence would be to insure that the revolt would keep going north, to Damascus and Aleppo and have this territory won by Arabs. In the midst of recruiting more Arabs for the march to Akaba, he notes in his pocket diary that he *"Can't stand another day here. Will ride N. & chuck it."* He drafted an unsent note to Clayton, telling him he is on his way to Damascus hoping to get killed. He did head off to the north to try and see what support the revolt does have, making it all the way to the outskirts of Damascus. He carries out important reconnaissance, studying the land and meeting tribal leaders. It was a remarkable journey. If Lawrence started out under tremendous stress, he was able to accomplish it in extremely dangerous circumstances. He made his

way back to Auda's camp by June 18th and wrote up his impressions for Clayton. By this time, Auda and Sherif Nasir had recruited 500 men and the larger force was ready to march on Akaba. They would move out and head generally in a western direction toward Bair. The Turks now were aware of an Arab force in the area and started to dynamite the wells. Lawrence and some of the men led a diversionary attack on the railway line. The Turks damaged some of the wells, not destroyed them, so the Arab force could still make repairs and carry on their advance. Additional blockhouses and stations were attacked and some bridges and culverts blown up.

The last real challenge before Akaba was the fortified pass of Aba el Lissan. Taking it would be difficult. It was through this valley that led the path to Akaba. By dawn, on July 2, the defending Turkish force was surrounded. The Turks were dug in well and for hours, the two sides were just sniping at each other. By noon, with the weather getting hotter, Lawrence insulted Auda by saying his men *"shoot a lot and hit a little."* Furious with the insult, Auda got 50 of his men and led a mounted cavalry charge on the Turkish position. Nasir and Lawrence quickly joined in on the flank, with a charge of four hundred men on camels. Coming down a slight slope in full charge, Lawrence fired away with his pistol, only to put the fifth shot through the head of his own camel, tumbling to the ground and briefly knocking himself out. When he came to, the attack was complete. It was a great success with over 150 Turkish prisoners captured and over 300 dead. Lawrence later wrote it up for the *Arab Bulletin* stating *"Auda himself (in front, of course) had a narrow escape, since two bullets smashed his field glasses, one pierced his revolver holster, three struck his sheathed sword, and his horse was killed under him. He was wildly pleased with the whole affair."* Satisfied with the victory, the Arabs wanted to attack the nearby Turkish stronghold of Ma'an, but Lawrence was able to persuade them that the town could be avoided and the task still rested on the capture of Akaba. The Arab force, many wearing captured Turkish tunics, continued their advance down through the valley. Additional skirmishes lead to more Turks surrendering. The force by now had grown to 1000 men and they were ready to make the final assault. On July 6,

in a driving sandstorm, the force reached Akaba, taking the town with little resistance. It was two months after they left Wejh.

With Akaba captured, immediate help was needed. There was little food and their numbers now included 600 Turkish prisoners. Lawrence and a small party of men headed off across Sinai to Suez. Arriving at the deserted British post of Shatt, opposite Suez, he had to deal with the frustrating military bureaucracy of getting transport to take him across the canal. Finally a right connection was made and a launch brought him quickly to the other side. Catching the train to Cairo, he went to see Clayton at once. Arrangements were immediately made to send the ship *Dufferin* to Akaba, loaded with supplies. Gold was needed too, for payment of the Arab troops. Lawrence learned that Allenby had replaced Murray as Commander-in Chief. Allenby was an active commander who now wanted an immediate assessment from Lawrence, of the Arab campaign. Lawrence was to meet Allenby before he could find a proper uniform for the one he left in Cairo was now moth eaten. At this meeting Lawrence explained to Allenby the importance of the revolt, the workings of the tribes, and what the Arabs could offer on the eastern edge of the Palestine front. Lawrence writes *"It was a comic interview, for Allenby was physically large and confident, and morally so great that the comprehension of our littleness was not easy to him. He sat in his chair looking at me – not straight, as is his custom, but sideways puzzled."* The Arab robed *"little bare-footed shirted person"* continued the lesson. Allenby *"did not ask questions, or talk much, but studied the map and listened to my explanations of the nature of eastern Syria and the inhabitants. At the end he put up his chin and said quite directly, 'Well, I will do for you what I can', and that ended it. "*

Jaafar Pasha. The affable Jaafar was Feisal's chief of staff and commanded the Regular Army. He stands with one of a number of Model T's that held up so well in the desert.

Makers plate removed from a wagon of the Hejaz Railway,
collected by Flying Officer V. D. Siddons of "X Flight." Siddons collection at the Royal Tank Museum.

Engine plate collected by Lawrence and given to his friend Vyvyan Richards.

-The Hejaz Railway-

On May 1, 1900, Sultan Abdul Hamid II announced the plans to build a railway from Damascus to Medina, a distance of over 800 miles. It was a railway line that would be used to primarily carry the Moslems making the pilgrimage to the holy Cities of Medina and Mecca. By tradition the pilgrims would start at Damascus and make their way south, along a centuries used caravan route. The difficult journey would take thirty to forty days. By providing rail transport, the travel time would be cut to four days. In addition to the religious reason given, the government was certainly aware of the military value of connecting by rail the far-distant cities in the south. Troops and supplies could be moved in and out quickly. Though the military potential is ignored in Turkish announcements, it is speculated upon from the very beginning in English and American press accounts of the building of the railway.

The financing of the railway project was supported in three major ways. Official Hejaz tax stamps were made. These would have to be purchased and affixed to almost all Ottoman legal documents. Government officials were made to make a 10% donation of one month's salary. Moslems from around the world were asked to make do-

nations towards the financing of the project. It was to be an all-Ottoman affair, built with money raised mostly by Moslems.

The French had an existing narrow gauge railway running from Damascus to Mezerib. The plan was to use this section and continue the railway south from Mezerib. Later, when the cost to purchase this section proved too much, it was decided to build a new line essentially parallel to the French line.

A ceremony celebrating the start of construction was held on October 26, 1900. Initially 3000 Turkish soldiers were employed to do the work. Three years of work on the railway would count as four years military service. Officers were given benefits based on how well their men performed. For the difficult stonework needed for bridge, tunnel and viaduct construction, large numbers of mostly Italian, Greek and Montenegrin workmen were brought in. As the railway got closer to the Holy Cities where foreigners were forbidden to go, the trained Turkish engineers took over the construction supervision.

Following the pilgrim caravan route took advantage of the stone water cisterns and reservoirs located along

Postcard illustrating a type of engine proposed for the Hejaz Railway.

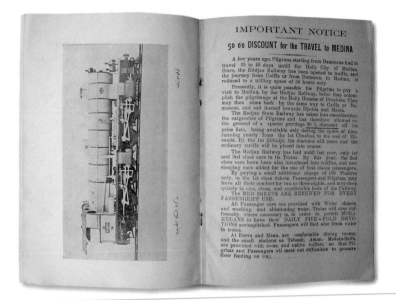

An interesting booklet advertising the Hejaz Railway for pilgrimage travel, printed in Constantinople 1913 with Turkish, English and Russian text. It illustrates the different classes of passenger cars, types of accommodations, and rates for travel.

Hejaz Railway Medal. The funding of the Hejaz Railway came from donations. Some of the donors were awarded medals. Others were presented with certificates. The medals came in gold, silver and nickel alloy. Most medals bear the date AH 1318. It is thought that the original medal ribbons were red or green.

the way. A workforce of this size needed a tremendous amount of food and water to sustain itself. A German engineer named Heinrich August Meissner supervised the construction and difficult logistics. The line proceeded south and for the next eight years slow, steady progress was made. On each September 1st, the anniversary date of the Sultan's accession to the throne, a new section of railway would be opened. By September 1902, the line reached Zarqa, 92 km. from Mezerib. An outbreak of cholera affected the construction but by September of 1903, the line now reached Deraa. One year later, the line was completed to Ma'an. By 1907 the line stretched 1000 km. to Al Ula, and was now taking pilgrims, a three-day journey by rail that would have taken three weeks by caravan. It was reported that 10000 pilgrims travelled by rail that year. By August of 1908, the railway line reached Medina and official opening celebrations were held on September 1st.

The local Bedouin tribes that had relied so heavily on escorting, taxing or raiding the pilgrims were angered by the new rail method of transporting them. It affected their livelihood. By 1911, attacks on stations, railway stock and track were growing and more Turkish troops had to be posted along the line. Travel by rail grew in numbers. In 1912, 30,000 pilgrims paid the 3.50-pound fare rather than the typical 40-pound caravan rate. By 1914, the number of pilgrims reached 300,000.

This narrow gauge track connected Damascus to Medina. During the Arab Revolt, it was this lifeline that the Arab raiders would continually disrupt. The strategy was to keep the line repairable so the garrison at Medina would get just enough supplies to stay and not be forced to make their way out. It was better to have 10000 troops confined than to escape and make their way north to assist the armies fighting Allenby.

When the railway was completed, it was looked on as an engineering marvel. The drop and rise in elevation was challenging. The long spans and heights of some of the bridges are just spectacular.

Today, sections of the Hejaz Railway have been restored and some steam locomotives still make runs, though now mostly for tourist groups. Railway museums are found in Damascus and Medina and some railway stations have been completely restored. Along the track, a few locomotives lay on their sides and stripped carriages can be seen, reminders of the war on the railway.

Raids on the Railway.

Allenby informed General Robertson, Chief of the Imperial Staff in London, how Lawrence's success could be used in helping define a strategy on the Palestine front. Allenby pushed the idea of Arab co-operation east of the Jordan River and how it would aid in shifting Turkish men and supplies away from his army. Robertson and the War Office endorsed the plan of Allenby making a push into Palestine by mid-September. After his meeting with Allenby, Lawrence knew his next move was to convince Feisal to move his army north to Akaba. Feisal and his army would work under Allenby, serving as his eastern flank, while he pushed on up to Jerusalem. Lawrence headed to Jidda to help convince King Hussein to transfer Feisal to Akaba and work under Allenby. The negotiations went more smoothly than anticipated and royal approval was given for the move north.

When Lawrence arrived back at Akaba, he was disturbed by the news that the Turks were trying to bribe Auda and the Howeitat over to their side. Frustrated by the slowness of

Turkish photograph showing a crew laying track near Ma'an, 1903. The steel sleepers used for most of the Hejaz Railway are clearly shown.

material and guns arriving at Akaba, Auda was considering the Turkish offer. Lawrence pointed out that Feisal and his armies were now on their way and British supplies and gold would be arriving soon. Auda's support was again assured.

British supplies did arrive. Feisal and Jaafar and their army came and immediately attention was given to fortify Akaba from an anticipated Turkish attack. The Turks were massing troops around Ma'an posing a threat. Air support was brought in and some bombing raids by Stent and his pilots put the Turks in disarray. Probing attacks by the Arabs kept them off guard as well. Soon Lawrence turned his attention to the railway.

Lawrence wanted to mine trains with an electronic detonator. He got some supplies from Egypt and sought out some technical advice from Captain Snagge of the *Humber*, now guarding Akaba. Snagge took an interest in Lawrence's activities and soon brought in his gunner warrant officer to help with the electrical circuits. Soon the group figured out a way of setting off the charge. Lawrence now had his detonators.

Lawrence chose the nearby station at Mudawara, eighty miles south of Ma'an. He brought along Howeitat and two English sergeants, Yells and Brooke, their specialty being the Stokes Mortar and the Lewis Gun. Lawrence started the group off slowly, this being the first time on camels for the sergeants. Leaving Akaba, toward Guweira and through the valley of Rumm, they finally approached the last crest overlooking the railway station. Closer inspection revealed it to be manned by 200 Turks, about twice the number with Lawrence. The raiding party pulled back for the night and would mine the line instead. The following morning, they headed south, looking for the perfect curve in the track for mine laying and a hill to provide covering fire. Lawrence found a two-arched bridge that was ideal. Being the first attempt with an electric mine, if there was difficulty in damaging the locomotive, the bridge itself would give way, causing the coach to derail.

While Yells and Brooke set up their Stokes Mortar and Lewis gun, Lawrence laid in 50 pounds of gelatine. It took

Fort at Medain Salih. The engine is a Krauss 0-6-0T.

Turkish photograph of the completed station at Deraa, 1903.

almost two hours just to lay the charge and cover all traces of disturbed ground. Final touches were made, duplicating the blown sand, by Lawrence fanning his cloak over the area. The wires stretched back two hundred yards back over the ridge, covered with exact care. The entire job took over five hours. Salim, Feisal's slave, asked for the honor of detonating the charge and several practice runs with a disconnected exploder were tried until he had it down perfectly. The raiding party retired for the evening, leaving a lookout.

The morning brought several small parties of Turks out from the station. There was fear that the charge would be discovered. Just as Lawrence decided it might be best to pack up and leave, the watchman cried out that a train was coming. Men were ordered into position. They would fire into the derailed carriages at 150 yards. Yells and Brooke took their positions at 300 yards. As the train made its way around the curve, Lawrence saw that it had two locomotives with ten box-wagons, crowded with troops. He quickly decided to fire the charge under the second engine and gave the signal to Salim. A loud roar went up with a cloud of smoke. Pieces of steel and iron ripped into the air including a large wheel of the locomotive that landed behind Lawrence and his men. The train was soon under attack by the rushing Bedouin, the Turks leaving the cars to escape the bullets of rifles and machine guns. Quickly the Stokes mortar was in action with deadly effect, landing shells where the Turks took shelter from the machine gun fire. The survivors dropped their equipment and ran, providing easy targets for the Lewis guns. This initial attack took ten

minutes and the Bedouin were now pillaging through the railway carriages. Lawrence walked down to see the damage the mine had caused. The small bridge was gone and a wagon had fallen into the gap. The following wagons were derailed, some damaged beyond repair. The second engine had its driving wheels blown off and was unrepairable. The first engine was not too damaged, but was derailed. In the meantime, the looting was going on madly. Anything of value was being grabbed; boxes ripped opened, items not wanted were smashed. Yells and Brooke surveyed the damage their weapons had caused and packed their gear. As the Arabs had their fill of loot, they retired. Soon Turks were leaving the station and making their way to the site of the attack and Lawrence and his group speeded up their departure, leaving some baggage camels and their kit. The raiding party suffered few losses and had ninety prisoners. As they made their way back through Rumm and Akaba, Lawrence realized that the railway was easily within reach for attack, with the armoured cars using the same route, going over the hardened ground to get to the line. On returning, the two British sergeants were wanted back in Cairo, Lawrence saying they could go away cheerfully, having won a battle single-handedly, survived dysentery, lived on camel's milk and learned to ride a camel fifty miles a day. Allenby, on Lawrence's recommendation, presented them with Distinguished Conduct Medals.

The devastating action had an effect on Lawrence and in two revealing letters written from Akaba, he shares his feelings. To his friend E.T.Leeds, 24 September 1917, Lawrence writes of how he destroyed a train with two engines but the killing of so many Turks truly bothered him.

I hope that when the nightmare ends I will wake up and become alive again. This killing and killing of Turks is horrible. When you charge in at the finish and find them all over the place in bits, and still alive many of them, and you know that you have done hundreds in the same way before and must do hundreds more if you can.

The mental toll these events were having on Lawrence was obvious. In a letter written the next day to Major Stirling, an officer that would soon join him at Akaba, Lawrence takes a different tone, appealing to the sport of it all. He records in detail the numbers of Turks killed and captured and how effectively the Lewis gun and Stokes mortar was used. He adds,

The Turks nearly cut us off as we looted the train, and I lost some baggage and nearly myself. My loot is a superfine red Baluch prayer-rug. I hope this sounds the fun it is. The only pity is the sweat to work theirs up, and the wild scramble while it lasts. It's the most amateurish, Buffalo Billy sort of performance, and the only people who do it well are the Bedouin. Only you will think it is heaven, because there aren't any returns, or orders, or superiors, or inferiors; no doctors, no accounts, no meals, and no drinks.

At Akaba, supplies were coming in but rather sporadically. Feisal had to be reassured by Joyce that the British support

Sherif Nasir, right, and Arab Regular Army officer at Shobek, north of Wadi Musa. Nasir was one of Feisal's best commanders. He was with the revolt from the beginning, played a leading role in the march to Akaba, attacked the railway numerous times and stayed active through the liberation of Damascus. With admiration Lawrence said Nasir fired the first and last shots of the Arab Revolt.

was indeed strong. The base at Akaba was also within striking distance of Turkish planes that would make annoying and ineffective bombing runs. Railway raids would continue and over the next few months, seventeen locomotives were destroyed by British and Arab parties working out of Akaba. Lawrence went to meet with Allenby in mid-October to set up a plan that would include an Arab military action, deep into Turkish territory. Allenby wanted Lawrence to destroy a railway bridge in the Yarmuk valley, over four hundred miles north of Akaba. This would cause a great diversion, while Allenby struck at Gaza and Beersheba. This Arab action, north into Syrian territory, also would weaken the post-war French political ambitions for the area.

Back at Akaba, Lawrence started planning for the attack, only to be frustrated by not getting all the supplies he needed. He set off on October 24th. His party included Indian machine gunners, assorted Arabs and bodyguards, Lieutenant Wood of the Royal Engineers and explosives expert, George Lloyd of the Arab Bureau, and Abd el Kader, grandson of the Algerian patriot and thought by some to be a Turkish spy. The party was beset by a variety of problems and bad luck. Before the planned attack, Abd el Kader disappeared. When the objective was finally reached, when Lawrence and his men were exploring where to set explosives, a rifle was dropped, alerting the Turkish sentries. The raiding party quickly retreated from the heavy rifle fire, with some of the troops dropping the explosives in their haste to leave. Lawrence was left with little material to do any damage so it was decided to blow up a train. The first attempt failed when the exploder failed to detonate. Lawrence sat behind a small bush, while the train slowly ran past, giving a small wave. The next day, with a fixed exploder, they destroyed a two-engine train, with parts landing near and over their heads because the shortage of wire obliged them to set up too close. A quick escape was needed as Turkish troops rushed out of the train. On the board was Jemal Pasha, heading down to Jerusalem to help defend it against Allenby. Letting down Allenby by not destroying the railway bridge, Lawrence and his raiding party headed back to the safety of Azrak Castle.

After days of story telling and rest at Azrak, Lawrence headed north with two companions, to Deraa, a main Turkish railway junction. He wanted to explore the town and immediate area. Wearing old peasant clothes, he thought he could observe first hand the defenses of the city and its roads. He was able to walk past the station and even reached the aerodrome when a Turkish sergeant challenged him. Lawrence was grabbed roughly by the arm and told that the Bey wanted him. With too many

An amazing document from Lawrence to General Clayton asking that no monetary charges be drawn against the kit lost by Brooke and Yells while taking part in the raid on the Mudawara Station. It shows the meticulous care that Lawrence took for his men. Walter Herbert Brooke and Charles Reginald Yells were called Stokes and Lewis in Seven Pillars of Wisdom.

Turks nearby it was useless to fight or flee. He explained that he was Circassian and excused from Turkish service. He was sent to the guardroom and asked to wash. Lawrence was brought to the Bey's room later in the evening, the subject for his homosexual attack. Resisting his advances, in the struggle Lawrence kneed him in the groin. The Bey ordered him beaten. Four men held him down while he was whipped and kicked. He then was dragged off by two men, each grabbing a leg and sexually abused. In this bloody state, he was brought back to the Bey who refused him. He was sent back to a room, washed and bandaged, and in the early morning managed to escape.

It was soon after the war that Lawrence recounted this terrible ordeal to his fellow officer, Colonel Stirling. He also wrote about it in graphic detail in his own book and shared further feelings about it with his close friend Charlotte Shaw, the wife of George Bernard Shaw. Whatever happened in Deraa deeply affected Lawrence, scarring him mentally, and allowing him to be physically degraded at times later in his life. He wrote to Charlotte Shaw,

For fear of being hurt, or rather, to earn five minutes' respite from a pain which drove me mad, I gave away the only possession we are born into the world with – our bodily integrity.

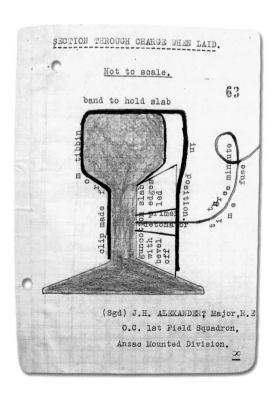

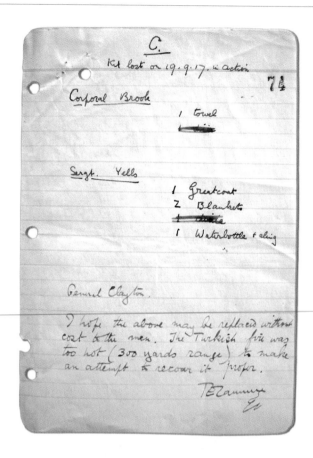

Lawrence made his way quickly back to Azrak, tired of the Arab war and his role in it. When he reached Akaba on December 3, Joyce wired Cairo expressing the need for Lawrence to meet with Clayton and General Staff to discuss further operations.

Lawrence was flown to the advance headquarters. Allenby's news was all good. Lawrence was informed of the success of the advance on Beersheba and the taking of Gaza. The army was within striking distance of Jerusalem itself. Lawrence's failure at Yarmuk was ignored. While at Allenby's headquarters, news came in that the Turks were withdrawing from Jerusalem and that the civilian authorities left in charge were surrendering to the British.

On December 11, at the invitation of Allenby, Lawrence was one of a limited number of staff members to take part in the official entry into liberated Jerusalem. He walked behind Allenby, wearing a borrowed uniform and hat. Lawrence described the entry has *"the most memorable event of the war, the one which, for its historical reasons, made a greater appeal than anything on earth."*

The capture of Jerusalem set the stage for the final push on Damascus. Allenby discussed with Lawrence

Drawing from the Arab Bureau archives detailing how to set a guncotton charge with a detonator on the Hejaz Railway. Eventually setting the charge was simplified by attaching the guncotton with wire.

THE PILGRIM-RAILWAY
Copyright

Photograph of the Hejaz Railway provided by Lawrence for Robert Graves to use in his biography Lawrence and the Arabs.

the need of bringing Feisal's forces north, up to the Dead Sea area, to proceed with Allenby's advance. Any serious advance further would have to wait until mid-February, when the supplies would be replenished. Allenby wanted the Arabs in control of the southern end of the Dead Sea, to protect his army from any attack from that direction, and prevent the Turks from getting food supplies from that area. Lawrence suggested that the Arabs could have control of all the land between

the Dead Sea and the railway by the middle of March.

Having some days of rest in Cairo allowed Lawrence to recharge and catch up with the political situation as well. Now aware of agreements being made between the British and French governments, the Turkish government was trying to dissuade the Arabs from siding with the allies. Lawrence would have some mending to do when he returned to Feisal at Akaba.

Captured Hejaz railway station photographed by Lt. E. H. Wade of the Hejaz Armoured Car Company.

British officers at Akaba. From left, around the table: Furness-Williams, Tookey, Langbeim, Peake, Ryde and Hornby.

-Troops with Lawrence-

In the first pages of *Seven Pillars of Wisdom*, Lawrence writes that his book is a personal narrative pieced out of memory, of his own role in the Arab Revolt.

> *My proper share was a minor one, but because of a fluent pen, a free speech and a certain adroitness of brains, I took upon myself, as I describe it, a mock primacy.*

Lawrence states that many of his comrades could each tell a like tale. He also states that his book, like all war-stories, is unfair to the unnamed rank and file.

Some of Lawrence's comrades did indeed write their own stories. W. F. Stirling, Earl Winterton and Hubert Young published magazine articles detailing their actions soon after the war. Each expanded these accounts into books. Fred Peake is quoted extensively in his biography *Arab Command* written by C. S. Jarvis. Alec Kirkbride wrote an important memoir of his own role as a young lieutenant in the Revolt. Recent books have covered the French troop involvement in the Hejaz and several others have focused on the role the air force played in the campaign.

Many Arab peoples and tribes participated in the revolt. However, a remarkable number of Allied men and units, often overlooked, played a supportive and important role, from all branches of service and with many ethnic backgrounds including a limited number of Egyptian, Indian, Gurkha, Algerian and Moroccan troops.

Hejaz Armoured Car Company

The Hejaz Armoured Car Company made a small but significant contribution to the Arab Revolt. Armoured cars had been used on the Western Front since early in the war. They had been effective in East Africa and were put to good use in the Senussi campaign in the Western Desert of Egypt.

Tom Beaumont, marked with an X, and others of the Hejaz Armoured Car Company. The man on the left wears a captured Turkish army belt and buckle. The officers and men display a casualness of uniform. Most men would eventually wear the Arab headdress on campaign.

Lt. E. H. Wade M.C. and his crew from the Machine Gun Corps
and Army Service Corps. Egypt, 1917.

Wade, 2nd from left, and other officers
on campaign in the Hejaz.

Two Rolls Royce armoured cars and crews arrived at Wejh in February 1917. Newcombe arranged for them to be tested in the country. Lieutenants Gilman and Wade were in command of the crews, made up of men from the Army Service Corps to drive and service the cars, and men of the Motor Machine Gun Corps to operate the guns. Lawrence states that having the Englishmen arrive at Wejh had an immediate effect because all of the food they had been eating was now declared medically unfit! He added,

> But the company of decent English people was a balancing pleasure, and the amusement of pushing cars and motor bicycles through the desperate sand about Wejh was great.

Gilman was able to modify the armour plating and completely strip it off the cars when a lighter load was needed to

get them across the softer sand. He also doubled up the tires to better get better support over ground. The drivers were challenged by the physical nature of the task and Lawrence said the men grew arms like boxers. This difficult breaking-in period would pay off when the unit was transferred north to Akaba where they arrived on November 1917. In addition to the Rolls cars, the Hejaz force had Crossley tenders from the Royal Flying Corps, which could carry a larger load. Talbot trucks were used to transport the 10 pounder mountain guns of the Royal Field Artillery detachment and smaller Model T Fords were found to be quite useful and could be lifted up and out of the soft sand when stuck.

The following information is from A History of the Transport Services of the Egyptian Expeditionary Force 1916-1917-1918 by G. E. Badcock:

Personnel and Equipment:

A Hejaz Armoured Car Battery consisted of 3 Officers, 23 Motor Machine Gun Corps other ranks, and 25 Royal Army Service Corps other ranks, 3 Rolls Royce armoured cars, and three Rolls Royce tenders. Talbots were tried as tenders, but proved unreliable. Early in 1918 the number of vehicles increased to 4 Rolls Royce armoured cars, 5 tenders, and 6 box Fords, all of which were quite satisfactory.

Type of Country:

From Akaba to the Nagb the country is practically desert. There are some remarkable mud flats near Nadana, some of which are seven to nine miles in extent and over which cars could travel at a very fast speed. In other parts, the country is mountainous and barren with deep wadis in which there is soft sand. In the neighborhood of Azrak there are lava fields covered with large black stones. The cars climbed all the hills except one near Nagb Eshgar, which as a long hill with a rise in parts of one in five, and up this cars were manhandled.

Duties:

The duties of these batteries consisted in carrying out reconnaissance over long distances, acting as escorts to Hejaz troops and demolition parties, and operating as a fighting unit against bodies of the enemy. Engagements took place several times with the enemy, chiefly at Tel Shahm, Mudawara and Jerdun. Many long journeys were undertaken by these batteries; on one occasion one of them, when acting as transport, did two complete journeys from Akaba to Azrak, a distance of 1200 miles. The farthest point north reached was Damascus.

Detail from a Harry Chase photograph, Guweira, April 1918. Lt. Gilman M.C., the officer in command of the Hejaz Armoured Car Battery, is seated on the nearest armoured car wearing an overcoat.

Detail of a Harry Chase photo, Gureira, April 1918. Armoured car and two Talbot trucks with mountain guns. Note the dog on the back of the armoured car.

Repairs:

There was no workshop attached and all repairs had to be done by the few fitters who accompanied the cars. Spare parts were carried in tenders, and once when a car broke down at Azrak a Handley Page flying machine was sent to the Advanced Base M.T. Depot, Ludd and brought back spare parts.

Loads Carried:

An armoured car carried:

1 Officer,

2 Gunners and 2 Drivers,

20 boxes of ammunition,

1 box of bombs,

Machine gun spares,

1 twelve-gallon fantassi (water tank),

2 two-gallon water cans

2 two-gallon oil cans,

2 or 3 cases of petrol,

2 or 3 boxes of gold (used to pay the Arabs.).

Sgt.T.W.Beaumont
Mine laying on Hejaz R.R.
Hallat Hamar - 1917
Temp. 130 degrees

Sgt. Tom Beaumont on the Hejaz Railway.

A tender carried:

2 Drivers,

2 Gunners (sometimes spare drivers and gunners),

4 fifteen-gallon fantassi,

5 cases of petrol,

4 two-gallon cans of lubricating oil,

Spare tires,

12 cases of ammunition, spare parts,

1 spare gun with tripod,

2 to 5 cases of gold.

Ten Pounder Section, Royal Field Artillery:

In addition to the ordinary armoured car batteries, a ten-pounder section, R.F.A., also operated in this country.

It consisted of 2 Officers and about 30 Other Ranks, R.F.A., and 12 R.A.S.C. Drivers and Fitters. The vehicles were 6 Talbot cars fitted with 2 ten-pounder mountain guns and 1 pom-pom.

Except for the difference in personnel and equipment, the experiences of this battery were the same as those of the armoured cars.

The armoured car batteries were very useful going over the hard grounds. Raids on the railway lines and on stations were carried out throughout the Hejaz campaign with attacks sometimes coordinated with Arab infantry and mounted troops. The units were even used in the final advance in September 1918 on Damascus. Lawrence entered Damascus in a Rolls Royce tender Blue Mist. Lawrence was quite taken by fighting with the armoured cars. He loved their speed and flexibility. He was also impressed by the mechanical skill and innovation of the force.

J.A.L. Brown and H. R. Green at machine gun practice, Wejh, 1917.
Photograph shows a stripped down armoured car in the background.

Firing practice with the 10 pd. mountain gun. The battery was commanded by Lt. Samuel Brodie with Lt. George Pascoe. The guns were used effectively in attacking the Hejaz Railway stations. Harry Chase photo, April 1918.

An exceptional panorama photograph by Harry Chase showing the armoured cars, Talbot trucks and crews of the Hejaz Armoured Car Battery. Lt. Gilmam is the first standing officer on the left, with Brodie and Pascoe standing in front of the Talbot truck.

'C' Flight, The Arabian Detachment

To assist the Arabs in the revolt, some kind of air support was needed. The Palestine front in general was getting second-rate machines. At best, as better planes arrived on the Western Front, the discarded, slower machines made their way out to Egypt. By November 1916, the revolt was underway with the seaport of Rabegh the major staging area for troop movement. The Arab troops had been bothered by the appearance of Turkish aeroplanes so they were reassured when Major A. J. Ross of the Royal Flying Corps, pilots, aircrew and four BE2c machines arrived. Lawrence spoke highly of Ross, *"an officer who spoke Arabic so well and was so splendid a leader there could be no two minds of the efficiency of his help."* Immediately work started to establish an aerodrome and landing ground. The base would include several Crossley tenders for reconnaissance. Support personnel included a few men from the Army Service Corps and the Royal Army Medical Corps. Total numbers of the Arabian Detachment was 12 officers and around fifty men.

By the end on November, daily reconnaissance flights were being taken. The duties would include taking aerial photographs to provide needed information on the terrain and troop location. The maps that were currently available had huge voids of unmapped territory.

Winter rains soon put a hamper on the number of flights taken, but by the end of January, "C Flight" could take aggressive action against the Turks. Bombing raids were carried out causing the Turks to shift some troops. These planes carried a limited number of bombs, usually eight to twelve, so the destructive capabilities of the raids were limited but still useful. Eventually additional landing grounds and refueling areas were established so the range of the flights could be increased. With the war shifting north and more attacks planned along the railway, the detachment was ordered to Yenbo. Major Ross pleaded the case to shift the aerodrome even further north, to Wejh. He won his point and by the end of March, the new base was established at Wejh with an added forward landing ground built about 100 miles east, closer to the railway. The weather itself was challenging, testing the ground crew to keep the planes operational. A particular problem brought on by the heat was the cracking of the engine cylinders.

On April 17, 1917, command of "C Flight" shifted from Major Ross to Captain F. W. Stent. He was a very personable officer who also spoke Arabic and had experience flying in the Sudan. By the end of the month, Stent was leading his pilots, including Captain Henderson and Lieutenant Siddons, on bombing raids attacking the

Some Royal Flying Corps officers of "C Flight", the Arabian Detachment of 14th Squadron.
Back row, l. to r: Lt. D. B. Aiken, 2Lt. V. D. Siddons, 2Lt. W. G. Stafford, 2Lt. J. M. Watson, 2Lt. J. D. Renfrew.
Front row, l. to r: Lt. W. L. Fenwick, Capt. T. Henderson, Commanding Officer Capt. F. W. Stent, Capt. W. N. Montgomery RAMC,
and Capt. F. H. V. Bevan.

Some of the same Royal Flying Corps officers on campaign in the Hejaz.
Back row, l. to r: Lt. W. L. Fenwick, Lt. J. M. Batting, Lt. V. D. Siddons,
the Royal Engineer officer Lt. R. G. Hornby, and Lt. W. G. Stafford.
Front row l. to r: The Machine Gun Corps officer in charge of the Hejaz Armoured Car Battery
Lt. L. H. Gilman, Capt. F. W. Stent, and Capt. T. Henderson.

Royal Flying Corps portable hangers at Rabegh, late 1916-1917. Under very difficult conditions,
the mechanics tried to keep the planes serviceable.

BE2c near Akaba. Joyce, the tall figure pictured on the right, coordinated the use of planes in support of the raids on the railway.

local railway stations. A frequent target was the larger station, track sidings and camp at El Ula. Bombing raids and additional aerial reconnaissance would continue with success until mid-July. When Akaba was captured on July 6 by Lawrence, Auda and the Howeitat, the war would shift north again. The role of "C Flight" had ended. By the end of July, "C Flight" was ordered packed up and returned to Egypt. Colonel Wilson cabled Captain Stent, *"Congratulations to yourself and Flight on excellent work performed in the Hejaz."*

Captain V. D. Siddons, center. Siddons flew with "C Flight" and later commanded "X Flight." After the war, he became a Methodist minister and during WW2 he served as a chaplain with the 8th Army.

"X Flight"

Lawrence had been assured of British help after the capture of Akaba. The Royal Navy was quickly bringing supplies and arms. With "C Flight", Lawrence had seen the value of air support in the southern Hejaz. He now wanted aeroplanes to support the Arab Northern Army of Feisal. He requested an air detachment to continue with the reconnaissance missions and the bombing of railway stations. Bombing attacks had already started on Ma'an, led by Captain Stent using an advance base. The pilots left Palestine with four days of rations, landed at the advance base to load up bombs and continued an intense attack on Ma'an and the Turkish base at Abu el Lissan. On September 9, a special detachment from 14th Squadron, under the command of Stent was sent to Akaba. Known as "X Flight" they would be under the orders of Lieutenant-Colonel P. C. Joyce. The detachment started with three B.E.12s and soon added two B.E.2es and one pusher plane, the D.H.2. The single seater B.E.12s carried a load of 12 to 16 bombs. The pilots continued to attack and bomb train stations and attempts were even made to coordinate the railway attacks with land forces.

In January 1918 Captain Furness-Williams took over command, replacing Stent. That month, three pilots working from an advanced landing ground, assisted Arabs in their attack on the railway station at Mudawara. Unfortunately, that day the ground troops could not overtake the Turks. Successful ground attacks, with air support, were carried out on stations in March and April. On April 19, Lieutenant-Colonel Dawnay led a mixed force of armoured cars and Arab troops on the station at Tel esh Shahin. To coordinate the attack with two aeroplanes, Dawnay's men communicated to the pilots using a code of wide strips of cloth laid on the ground, ordering to bomb at once. The attack was successful. Great assistance was made in continuing the aerial photo reconnaissance work. The pilots were also used to shuffle Lawrence and others quickly to headquarters and back, to plan strategies, travelling in hours over land that could have taken a full day or more.

In June, "X Flight" was moved inland from Akaba to El Gueira. Captain Siddons took over command. A Nieuport plane had been added recently to the flight and a Bristol Fighter would come in August. Occasional aerial combat would happen, but most work was still in bombing runs and aerial photography. In August, planes were used to assist Buxton and his men of the Imperial Camel Corps in attacking and capturing the station of Mudawara. By perfectly timing the bombing of the Turkish redoubt, many British casualties were avoided.

By September, the final push on Damascus would start. Superior British control of the skies led to effective bombing of the main railway stations including Deraa.

Captain F. H. Furness-Williams, Commanding Officer of "X Flight," in his Nieuport 17. The famous ace Billy Bishop flew this particular Nieuport B 1566 on the Western Front from April through July 1917. While piloting this plane, Bishop made 33 of his claimed victories. Arriving to "X Flight" in the fall of 1917, the Nieuport was used until the end of the war.

Another view of B 1566.

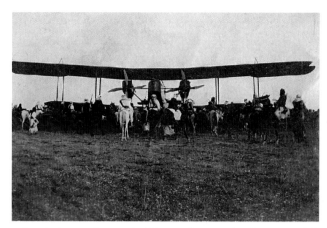

The only known photograph of the Handley Page bomber surrounded by Arab troops at Um el Surab. Photograph taken by Lt. E. H. Wade of the Hejaz Armoured Car Battery.

Lawrence wanted and got even more air support. The Northern Army was still being harassed by the occasional German plane, machine gunning and bombing the men. Bristol Fighters of No 1 Squadron of the Australian Flying Corps came to support. On September 17, Lawrence and his men were near the Hejaz Railway line south of Deraa when they were surprised by eight planes sent from the German aerodrome just four miles away. The party was bombarded for over an hour. Soon Lieutenant H. R. Junor of "X Flight" arrived on the scene, flying his BE 12a, *"a type so out of date that it was impossible for fighting and little use for reconnaissance."* Junor engaged the enemy while Lawrence, Young, Peake and their troops looked on. Lawrence continues, *"We watched with mixed feelings, for the hopelessly old fashioned machine made him cold meat for any of the enemy scouts or two-seaters: but at first he astonished them, as*

he rattled in with his two guns. They scattered for a careful look at this unexpected opponent. He flew westward across the line and they went in hot pursuit, with that amiable weakness of aircraft for a hostile machine, however important the ground target. We were left in perfect peace." Soon Junor returned, flying for his life, with three planes in hot pursuit. Running out of petrol, he brought the plane to the ground on an improvised landing strip cleared by Young and his men. A gust of wind caused the plane to flip on landing but Junor quickly unbuckled and removed his plane's machine guns. Soon after, a well-placed German bomb destroyed the plane. Junor anxiously took his guns and secured a Ford car and helped assist on destroying the railway, now as a foot soldier, not an airman.

On September 22, the famed pilot Ross Smith landed the huge Handley Page bomber at Um el Surab, bringing

Junor and his aircraft.

Junor's crashed BE12a, before it was destroyed by a bomb. Junor stripped the guns and joined on raids against the railway. September 16, 1918

needed petrol for the Bristol Fighters and armoured cars. The arrival caused great excitement among the Arabs. Lawrence writes that to the Arabs this was THE aeroplane, of which the other smaller planes were just foals. The mounted Arabs circled around the bomber, firing rifles into the air. Two nights later, the Handley Page would attack Mafrak station. Lawrence and his men would hear the explosions and see the flashes. British bombing attacks would continue to cause mass destruction with devastating losses to the retreating Turkish armies. On the morning of October 1st, soon after its capture by Arab troops and Australian cavalry, British planes would land in Damascus.

Stuart Reid's painting of the landing of the Handley Page, piloted by Ross Smith, at Um el Surab, September 22, 1918.

French Troops in the Hejaz

Lawrence certainly had strong feelings about keeping the French out of the Hejaz politically. If the Arabs couldn't get independence, second best would be under British guidance and the worst, he felt, under French dominance. This soon was out of his control with the signing of the Sykes-Picot Agreement where both British and French governments agreed to their sphere of influence in the region.

The French did have troops in Palestine and the Hejaz. The commander of the French Military Mission to the Hejaz was Colonel Edouard Bremond. Lawrence called him the only true soldier in the Hejaz, no doubt paying attention to his professional military training at St. Cyr and his distinguished work in Morocco since 1907. Bremond wanted a mixed French and British force to land in Hejaz at Rabegh to prevent a Turkish assault on Mecca. He had no faith in a guerrilla war, felt the Bedouin were too easy to buy off and influence, and that the war could only succeed by using a trained regular army. Bremond also opposed any nationalist Arab movement. Lawrence favored a pure Arab movement with Feisal leading an Arab army moving north from Yenbo to Wejh, its long-range goal being the taking of Damascus. Bremond's plan was ignored, and the British backed Feisal with arms and gold. By January, Feisal was moving north to Wejh. Bremond published his account of the campaign *Le Hedjaz dans la Guerre Mondiale* in 1931, letting it be known his bitter feelings toward Lawrence.

The French still maintained a small military presence in Hejaz of one thousand men. The French troops were Muslim colonial troops from Morocco, Algeria and Tunisia, with mostly French officers. By August 1917, this force was reduced to 500 men divided up between the Arab Army of the North under Feisal's command, the Army of the East under Abdullah's command, and the Army of the South under Ali's command.

The brave Algerian Captain Raho of the 2nd Regiment of Spahis and his detachment of forty men led a series of raids against the Hejaz Railway, starting in February 1917. In March, Lawrence joined Raho in a raid on the station at Aba el Naam. Along with Garland and Newcombe, he and his men destroyed many bridges and rails in the southern Hejaz. Up until October 1918, Raho continued leading successful raids around Medina.

Working closely with Lawrence out of Akaba was Captain Rosario Pisani and his Algerian mountain artillery. Pisani was a veteran of the Moroccan campaigns, having served with Bremond. Lawrence thought of him as a very brave soldier, but always anxious to add more medals to his chestful. Pisani organized railway raids with his mule-borne detachment of small 65 mm Schneider mountain guns. He and his men also made coordinated attacks with the armoured cars. Lawrence himself recommended Pisani for the Military Cross

Colonel Edouard Bremond, head of the French Military Mission, (third from left) with Commandant Cousse on his left. Cousse succeeded Bremond. The Dominican priest Antonin Jaussen is also present. A famed archaeologist, Jaussen was active in the Intelligence Department in Jerusalem, working with the British and French. Before the war, Jaussen travelled the area extensively, getting to know many of the tribes and leaders. In 1909, his book Coutumes des Arabes Pays de Moab *was published. He and Rafael Savignac had recently published* Mission Archeologique En Arabie.

Captain Pisani and some of his officers with Feisal and Nesib el Bekri. The Arab officer standing behind Feisal and Pisani is identified by Lawrence as Fejid el Khajen and the seated Arab officer as Selim Kalbage.

for *"brilliant conduct and excellent services rendered during the course of operations against the Hejaz railway."*

For the mid-September 1918 push north on Deraa, Pisani would lead his 140 men, assisting in the capture of Tell Arar and the station at Mezerib, and providing needed artillery support on several more important occasions, leading to the capture of Damascus. Pisani would accompany Feisal and Lawrence to the Peace Conference at Versailles.

Pisani with his Mountain Artillery prepare to advance.

French 65 mm. mountain gun in action.

Overlooking Maan, Pisani (right) and Jaafar (center) observing the Mountain Artillery.

French Mountain Artillery in camp at Guweira. Examples of the 65mm and 80mm guns can be seen with the ammunition and equipment fitted for mules.

British Officers with Lawrence

Lawrence and staff at Akaba.

Lawrence, seated in the center, wears a paisley patterned robe and a dark abayeh. He is seated on a "Roorkhee Chair," a popular piece of campaign furniture. A portable gramophone and a box of records show his love of music. The officers are certainly enjoying each other's company in this staged but relaxed photograph. Standing left to right: Sub-Lieutenant Langbeim of the Royal Naval Reserve in a khaki service tunic. Captain H. C. Hornby, an explosives expert of the Royal Engineers who also led raids against the Hejaz Railway, wears a drab service tunic bearing the ribbon of the Military Cross. Major W.E. Marshall of the Royal Army Medical Corps, sometimes tent mate of Lawrence and known as the "fighting bacteriologist" wears a tropical service tunic. He won the Military Cross on the Western Front and would stay on in the Hejaz until the end of the campaign. Seated left to right: Major P.G.W. Maynard of the Royal Irish Rifles and a veteran of the Boer War, recently appointed staff officer to Colonel Joyce. Major Scott of the Royal Inniskilling Fusiliers, base commander at Akaba, is wearing a cuff rank drab tunic and holds a terrier named "Robert." Captain Raymond Goslett of the Royal Army Service Corps is seated on Lawrence's camel saddle petting a saluki named "Shorter."

Ramsay of the Royal Army Medical Corps (left) and Dowsett of the Machine Gun Corps and the Hejaz Armoured Car Company (right) with Madame Auda abu Tayi.

Dawnay and men of the Hejaz Armoured Car Company. Dawnay wears the tropical service tunic of the Coldstream Guards.

British officer's tropical service dress tunic with bandolier for .303 ammunition, pistol holster, compass and map case. There were no official regulations enforced for uniforms worn by officers in the Hejaz. Most men wore a practical combination of British and Arab clothing.

Captain Norman Willis Clayton with servant. Clayton, a Machine Gun Corps officer, won the Military Cross on the Western Front. He was sent to the Hejaz to help train Egyptian troops.

Captain Hornby of the Royal Engineers with Arab guide. Hornby and Newcombe were very active in destroying the Hejaz Railway.

Herbert Garland (1882-1921).

Herbert Garland was born in Sheffield on 10th November 1882. Little is known about his early schooling but in 1901 he enrolled as a Private in the Royal Military Academy, Army Ordnance Corps, at Woolwich. He was posted to Guernsey. In 1906, with a rank of 2nd Corporal, he was transferred to Khartoum. While in the Sudan, he was able to get his romantic novel *Diverse Affections* published in England. With the rank of Sergeant, he left the Army Ordnance Corps in 1913. While living in Cairo at this time, Garland developed a strong interest in metallurgy. He became a member the Institute of Metals and the Society of Chemical Industry. Garland was appointed Superintendent of the Explosives Laboratory and Magazines at the Citadel. He studied Ancient Egyptian metal casting techniques and wrote several articles published in archeological journals of the time.

In early 1915, Garland designed a type of simple mortar and grenade that were soon produced in large quantities for the Gallipoli campaign. Not much more than a simple pipe mounted on a board that could be adjusted at a required angle, the mortars were needed weapons to propel simple bombs into the Turkish trenches. One of these mortars is preserved at the Australian War Memorial.

In October 1916, Garland was sent to Wejh and Yenbo to train Arabs in explosives. Wingate was aware of Garland's love of blowing things up and with his knowledge of Arabic, he would be the perfect teacher for these willing pupils. Lawrence wrote to Hogarth endorsing Garland for the job he was soon doing:

Garland in the Hejaz.

Garland is much more use than I could be. For one thing, he is senior to me, and is an expert on explosives and machinery. He digs their trenches, repairs their guns, teaches them musketry, machine gun work, signaling: gets on with them exceedingly well, always makes the best of things, and they all like him too.

He perfected techniques used for mining the railway and was the first British officer to attack the Hejaz line. He instructed Lawrence on how to use the demolition equipment. Lawrence himself describes Garland's work best, In *Seven Pillars* he writes:

Garland was an enquirer in physics, and had years of practical knowledge of explosives. He had his own devices for mining trains and felling telegraph and cutting metals, and his knowledge of Arabic and freedom from the theories of the ordinary sapper-school enabled him to teach the art of demolition to unlettered Bedouin in a quick and ready way. Incidentally, he taught me to be familiar with high explosives. Sappers handled it like a sacrament; but Garland would shove a fistful of detonators into his pocket, with a string of primers, fuse, and fusees, and jump gaily on his camel for a week's ride to the Hejaz Railway. His health was poor, and the climate made him regularly ill. His heart was weak, and troubled him after any effort or crisis: but he treated these risks as freely as he did detonators, and persisted until he had derailed the first train and broken the first culvert in Arabia.

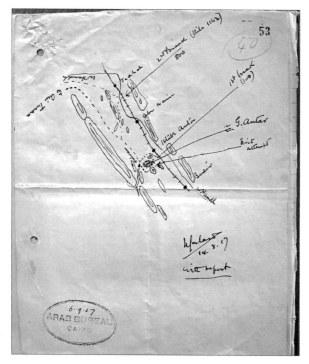

Map sketched by Garland illustrating his report to the Arab Bureau of his raids near Abu Na'am and Istabl Antar stations, August, 1917.

Garland would stay in the southern Hejaz while Lawrence and Feisal moved north to Akaba. While leading his Arabs on railway raids, he was frustrated by their effort and began to doubt if any regularly trained officer could lead them effectively. In his written reports for the Arab Bureau, he gave detailed notes perfecting how to place charges and be most effective in damaging the railway. His health remained an issue and he suffered from bouts of dysentery, fatigue and dyspepsia. Garland stayed on in the Hejaz and accepted the surrender of Fakhri Pasha of Medina, who was reluctant to surrender to an officer of Captain Garland's low rank. Garland returned to Cairo and served as Acting Director of the Arab Bureau and edited the final issues of the *Arab Bulletin*.

Garland in Arab robes about to embark on a railway raid.
Garland never got comfortable wearing Arab robes and complained with humour that corners of his keffiyeh would keep flying up, flicking the cigarette out of his mouth.

He resigned his commission in May 1920. His health problems turned even more serious. He arrived in England 27 March 1921 and was admitted to Gravesend Hospital on the 30th. He died three days later. Garland was buried in an unmarked grave at Gravesend Cemetery. In 2004, Garland's daughter, Mena O'Connor of Rhode Island, less than two years old when her father died, located the unmarked grave and placed a tombstone over it.

Garland on camel.

Frederick Peake (1886-1970).

Peake was educated at Stubbington House, Fareham and the Royal Military College, Sandhurst. He was commissioned into the Duke of Wellington's Regiment in 1906. He joined the 1st Battalion in India. He occupied much of his time studying the local languages and going hunting. At his own request, he transferred to the Egyptian Army in 1913. At the start of the war, many commissioned officers serving with the Egyptian Army tried to get back to their original regiments to serve at the front. Peake's commanding officer was able to do this while he was unsuccessful, now left in charge of his Egyptian Battalion in the Sudan. Peake's troops were active in fighting Abyssinian slave raiders and would have a role in the Senussi campaign in Darfur. By 1916, with extended leave due, Peake made his way to Cairo and secured a position with the Commanding Officer of 17 Squadron, Royal Flying Corps. He went to Salonika for the next five months as an Observer and Wind Adjutant. He soon received official notice to return to the Egyptian Army and to explain himself why his leave was extended by two months. When Peake's explanation of events was accepted, he was sent back to Darfur to the Camel Corps. The next year he had a run of bad health including severely hurting his neck with a fall from a camel. He suffered from a liver abscess and was sent back to England to recover. Coming back to Egypt, his ship was torpedoed off Alex-

Peake in the service dress worn while serving with Lawrence. Photograph from Arab Command by C. S. Jarvis.

andria, but was able to bob in the sea with a beer and some sandwiches until he was rescued.

By early 1918, Peake was appointed command of the Egyptian Camel Corps Company at Beersheba. By April, this group was transferred to Akaba to be part of Feisal's Northern Army. Soon they were taking part in raids on the Hejaz Railway supporting the armoured car units. Their first attack was with Dawnay, Lawrence and Hornby on the station of Tel Shahm. Organized by Dawnay, with the timed precision of the Guards officer he was, Peake urged his Camel Corps on and the station was taken. Lawrence grabbed the station bell and Peake took the ticket punch, followed by Bedouin looting the stored rifles and ammunition. Peake soon had his Egyptians trained in the art of railway demolition. By the push to Deraa in the fall of 1918, they were damaging extensive portions of the line. Peake and Lawrence perfected the "tulip technique" where placing the charge under the sleeper would cause the explosion to lift the sleeper up and bend the metal, not break it, distorting the rail, making it impossible for the Turks to repair. The men earned the sobriquet 'Peake Demolition Co Ltd.'

Camel saddle used by Peake.
The saddle of Imperial Camel Corps pattern with Citadel Egypt and War Department stamps and markings.

At early morning on 17 September, with the advance needing a final push to stay on Allenby's schedule, Lawrence arrived at camp anxiously wanting the day's demolition to start. He came across Peake enjoying a full breakfast *'with a certain amount of shiny plate and a box of Corona cigars.'* Lawrence was stunned, caught off guard by the need of the Egyptian troop to get a good meal before a hard days work. Lawrence wrote,

I wanted the whole line destroyed in a moment: but things seemed to have stopped. The army had done its share...but why was there no demolition going on? I rushed down to see, and found Peake's Egyptians having breakfast. It was like Drake's game of bowls, and I was dumb with admiration: but they did not know they were magnificent, and so gained no merit.

Peake and his men continued their effective work until the fall of Damascus.

After the war, Peake stayed in Transjordan and raised the Arab Legion. He became a close friend of Emir Abdullah. He retired in 1939 leaving the command of the Arab Legion to Glubb Pasha. Though Peake originally planned to write his autobiography, C. S. Jarvis used his notes for his biography of Peake titled *Arab Command*.

Peake's valise bag used while in command of the Egyptian Camel Corps and one of his agals.

Peake on camel identified on the photograph by Lawrence.

Walter Francis Stirling (1880-1958).

Stirling spent much of his youth at Hampton Court Palace where Queen Victoria had set up housing for young Naval widows and their families. He attended the Royal Military College, Sandhurst and was commissioned into the Royal Dublin Fusiliers in 1899. His first active service was in the 2nd Boer War with his regiment as part of the Natal Field Force. He was attached to the 4th Division Mounted Infantry in Dundonald's Brigade, and later appointed Adjutant with the 14th Mounted Infantry. He took part in the relief of Ladysmith. Lord Kitchener notified him of his award of the Distinguished Service Order *"for skill and gallantry in action at Kafferspruit 19 Dec. 1901."*

Stirling joined the Egyptian Army in 1906 serving with the 11th Sudanese Regiment. In 1912 he retired from the army and went to Canada. He soon returned to Egypt taking up duties as Secretary of the Khedival Sporting Club in Cairo. At the outbreak of war, he did various assignments in Egypt including being trained as an observer in the Royal Flying Corps. This led to flying opportunities over the Sinai and included a crash landing in the desert.

Stirling rejoined his old regiment, the Royal Dublin Fusiliers, who had suffered severe causalities at the landings on Gallipoli. He served as second in command of the 1st Battalion for three months.

Returning to Egypt he was appointed Intelligence Officer at General Murray's headquarters at Ismailia. It was here that he

Stirling in Egypt soon after the war. Stirling was an animal lover and shared a strong interest in Arabian horses with Feisal.

LIEUTENANT-COLONEL W. F. STIRLING, D.S.O., M.C.

Miniature medals belonging to Stirling. The miniatures would be worn with "mess dress" on formal dining occasions.

met T. E. Lawrence. Stirling stayed active on Allenby's staff, assisting in the Third Battle of Gaza and in the operations around Jerusalem. Stirling was awarded the Military Cross for his services and this was presented to him by the Duke of Connaught during his official visit to the newly liberated city of Jerusalem.

Dawnay arranged for Stirling to join the Hejaz force in June 1918. Lawrence described his as *'a skilled Staff Officer, emollient and wise,'* whose *'passion for horses was a passport to intimacy with Feisal and the chiefs.'* Over the next months, he worked closely with Lawrence, Jaafar, and Nuri going with them on many raids. He rode into Damascus with Lawrence and would stay on as an advisor to Feisal. For his actions in the Hejaz, Stirling was awarded a bar to his Distinguished Service Order. The citation reads, *'For gallant service rendered during the operations resulting in the occupation of Damascus by the Arab forces. By his example and personal courage whilst leading the Arabs, he, in conjunction with another officer, was* mainly instrumental in securing the successful operation of the town, and the establishment without grave disorder of the Arab military authorities therein.'

Stirling was also awarded the Order of Al Nahda, Second Class, by King Hussein of the Hejaz, for his contributions towards the success of the Arab Revolt.

After the war, Stirling held a number of administrative posts in Egypt and Palestine and was briefly military advisor in Albania. He served on the staff with the British forces in Syria during World War II, and survived a post-war assassination attempt. He retired to Egypt and Tangier. While in Morocco, he renewed his friendship with James McBey, an official war artist of the Palestine campaign. Stirling's autobiography *Safety Last* is an exciting recounting of his varied career. He defends Lawrence and adds that he *'took the limelight from those of us professional soldiers who were fortunate to serve with him.'*

Stirling, taken at Damascus,
the day he entered the city with Lawrence.

Stewart Francis Newcombe (1874-1956).

Newcombe was born at Brecon and educated at Christ's Hospital and Felsted. He attended the Royal Military Academy at Woolwich gaining the distinction of 100 percent marks in mathematics. He was also awarded a Sword of Honour. He was commissioned into the Royal Engineers and took part in the 2nd Boer War with Mounted Infantry operations. Newcombe joined the Egyptian Army in 1901 and served with them until 1911. His work was primarily with the Sudan Railways, doing survey work in the laying of new lines. In 1913 and early 1914, he was the surveying officer mapping the Sinai Peninsula, working with Lawrence and Woolley.

At the start of the war, Newcombe went to France. After the entry of Turkey, Newcombe was assigned to Egypt to the Intelligence Department. He travelled to Cairo with Lawrence. He was to be Gilbert Clayton's assistant. Working closely with Aubrey Herbert, George Lloyd, Leonard Woolley and Lawrence, they became known as the 'Five Musketeers.' Newcombe joined the Allied forces at Gallipoli from September 1915 until January 1916 attached to the 2nd Australian Division. He earned the Distinguished Service Order. His citation for the award reads: "For conspicuous gallantry and devotion to duty near Anzac, Gallipoli Peninsula, on 29 Oct. 1915. During rescue operations he entered a mine tunnel soon after the first causalities were reported, and although suffering from the effects of fumes, he continued to lead rescue parties till he was completely disabled by the gas. One officer lost his life on this occasion in the attempt at rescue." After Gallipoli, Newcombe went to the Western Front. He was appointed to the Sherif of Mecca's forces at the end of 1916, working again with Lawrence. Newcombe actively took up railway demolition. Leading a small force of Arabs, dressing the part in Arab robes, Newcombe was relentless in his energy to the task. Lawrence writes,

Newcombe in Arab costume.

He did four times as much as any Englishman would have done and 10 times as much as the Arabs thought necessary!

In June 1917, as part of the plan to take Beersheba, Newcombe led a diversionary force of 70 camel corps, cutting telegraph lines and disturbing activities. This forced the Turks to move a large number of troops to the area east of Sheria to deal with him. Though taking pressure off Allenby's main force, Newcombe's men were severely outnumbered. After making a strong initial defense, he lost twenty men with more wounded, and was forced to surrender.

Orders and medals of Newcombe including the Distinguished Service Order won at Gallipoli, the French Legion d'Honneur, the Italian Order of the Crown, and the pre-war earned Turkish Order of Osmanieh.

Newcombe was taken to Turkey as a prisoner of war. While there, with the aid of a French woman, Mlle. Elsie Chaki, he was able to escape. After the war, Newcombe would marry Elsie. They would have a son and a daughter. Their son, in honour of T. E. Lawrence, was christened Stuart Lawrence. Lawrence also was the boy's godfather. Newcombe kept up a strong interest in Middle Eastern affairs and even in 1940 was making official trips into Syria. He was an active member of the Palestine Exploration Society and the Royal Central Asian Society. When he passed away, he was remembered for his hatred of pomp and pomposity.

He was unassuming, accessible, sound and scrupulously fair, if stern, in his judgements and advice, to men of all races and of all ranks. Those of his own Corps and others who served above or below him in war and peace, will always remember his driving power on any job, his audacity and boldness in conception and execution, his wonderful capacity for friendship and the love of fun and unfailing cheerfulness which merely increased when difficulties arose.

Newcombe and Lawrence remained strong friends. Newcombe was one of the six pallbearers at his funeral service.

Pierce Charles Joyce (1878-1965).

Joyce was born in Mervue, Galway, Ireland, and the son of Pierce J. Joyce, Deputy-Lieutenant for the region. His family was very active socially and sponsored various racing and fox hunting events. He was educated at Beaumont College, Old Windsor.

Joyce joined the First Battalion The Connaught Rangers in 1900 and went with his regiment to South Africa during the 2nd Boer War. He actively participated in operations in the Transvaal and the Orange River Colony. He was severely

Joyce in service dress uniform of the Connaught Rangers, 1919.

wounded in action, leaving him with a rather stiff walk.

Joyce joined the Egyptian Army in 1907 and in early 1910, took part in the Atwot campaign against the Dinka tribe on the Upper Nile. He was awarded the Fourth Class Order of the Medijie for his services. In the Sudan, his work gained the attention of Sir Reginald Wingate and Sir Gilbert Clayton.

Joyce, in charge of an Egyptian detachment of 450 men, arrived in the Hejaz in late 1916. He was to help with defending Rabegh. Joyce was not impressed with the fighting quality of the Arab troops and he felt certain they would run away if the Turks attacked. Fortunately, the anticipated attack never materialized.

Joyce (center) with Gilman and an armoured tender. Note the mounted machine gun in the back of the tender.

Akaba was captured in July 1917. British ships started landing supplies. By August, Jaafar and his army arrived. HMS *Humber* would be guard ship over the coastal town. British advisors and a small contingent of troops landed with Major Joyce in command of the base. Immediately Joyce tended to the needs of his men, ordering everything from much needed small arms ammunition to the recreationally wanted footballs. Joyce was also convinced that any military success with the Arab forces rested with them being trained as a traditional trained professional army. Joyce was able to get uniforms and equipment too for Jaafar's troops. But Joyce was more than a camp commandant. He actively took part in railway raids, attacking stations and destroying rail and bridges.

Clayton made it clear to Lawrence that Joyce was in charge of the Hejaz operations. Tensions were raised when Lawrence would take the unconventional way to warfare that the professional soldier Joyce would sometimes object to. However, both men had great respect for each other. Lawrence enjoyed the broad, six foot four inch Irishman's humour and outlook on life. Lawrence wrote that

he was a man in whom one could rest against the world: a serene, unchanging, comfortable spirit.

When Lawrence went around Joyce's back and planned out the Mudawara raid using the Imperial Camel Corps, Joyce had to be calmed down and reassured by Colonel Dawnay that communication between all parties would be improved and Joyce would be kept informed of all plans. The mostly smooth nature of their work led to the military success of the revolt, with Lawrence handling the Bedouin armies with Joyce supervising the duties of the regular Arab army, the armoured car batteries and air support.

For his services in the Hejaz, Joyce received the Distinguished Service Order, and from the King of the Hejaz, the Second Class Order of Al Nahda. As personal thanks of the campaign, Lawrence presented Joyce with his silver decorated camel pommels. After the war, Joyce served as military advisor to Iraq, working with his friends King Feisal, Jaafar and Nuri Said. He went on retired pay in 1932. Unfortunately, Joyce wrote very little about his own career, though there are transcripts of his talk given on the BBC about T. E. Lawrence when he spoke highly of Lawrence's bravery and his strong admiration of him. Much of Joyce's Hejaz correspondence is in the collection of the Liddell Hart Centre for Military Archives of King's College, London.

Joyce and British officers. Back row, left to right: Greenhill, Young, unidentified, Bamford.
Seated, left to right: Ramsey, Gilman, Joyce, unidentified. In front: Grisenthwaite

Imperial Camel Corps

The Imperial Camel Corps was formed in early 1916, made up of companies of men from the United Kingdom, Australia, and New Zealand. Under the command of Brigadier General C. L. Smith VC., they participated in the campaigns in the Western Desert, across the Sinai, the attacks on Gaza, the capture of Jerusalem and the advance on Amman. Using the camels for transport, the men fought as mounted infantry. The advantage of being borne on camels was that the men could pursue the enemy over the desert terrain. The hard ground of Palestine no longer required camel troops. The Lighthorse would be more useful. By the spring of 1918, Allenby's campaign had slowed and many men were shifted from his army and sent to France as needed reinforcements. It was decided to disband the Imperial Camel Corps and keep only the 2nd Battalion, made up of soldiers from English yeomanry units.

The break up of the Camel Corps provided a chance for Lawrence to put in his claim for two thousand camels for the Hejaz Army. In addition to the gift of the camels, Allenby agreed to a plan to use 300 men of the remaining Camel Corps in a series of raids in the Hejaz. Lawrence and Dawnay, Allenby's chief of staff and liason officer for the Hejaz, conceived of a plan of sending these men deep into the Hejaz, capturing the railway station at Mudawara and proceeding North, destroying more rail, bridges and tunnels. This English group would be the largest of the foreign troops used in the Hejaz, an action resisted earlier because of the possible ill feeling that might be aroused among the Arabs. It was agreed that the use of the English troops

Officer of the Imperial Camel Corps.

would be independent from the Hejaz army. It was also necessary for the Turkish command to know that English troops were now well into their territory. This would have an effect of pulling troops away from Allenby's army west of the Jordan River.

Commanding the Imperial Camel Corps was Robin Buxton, a veteran of Gallipoli. He was an Arabic speaker and served in the Sudan Civil Service before the war. He was educated at Eton and Trinity College, Oxford and would get along quite well with Lawrence.

Buxton led his 300 men across Sinai and arrived in

A British officer and an armoured car crew make way for the Imperial Camel Corps.
At least one crew member finds comfort in the shade of the armoured car.

Akaba on July 30th. Lawrence met the troops there and addressed the men personally. The soldiers were quite taken by Lawrence speaking to them directly and so candidly. He warned them of the dangers ahead, the planned thousand-mile march in less than a month, and the challenges they would face working with Arab allies.

Lawrence accompanied the men through Wadi Rum on their way to the station at Mudawara. While he headed back to Akaba, Buxton and his men prepared for the early morning assault on the station. Doing reconnaissance work using Talbot trucks of the 10-pounder battery, Buxton, Stirling and Marshall planned the attack. At dawn, August 8th, the Camel Corps attacked the station. Meeting little resistance, the southern redoubt was quickly taken. The northern redoubt would be a tougher fight. Brodie and his mountain guns were brought in. Coordinated air support from

DEMOLITIONS ON THE RAILWAY
Copyright

Imperial camel corps . 1918

*Harold Brown, Lewis Gun Section,
No. 10 Company, Imperial Camel Corps.
Brown, in full marching order with a bandolier of
Lee-Enfield ammunition. On one side of the camel
is a 50-pound bag of dhurra, on the other
is a fantassi, a water tank holding about five
gallons. Around the camel's neck is an agal,
used for tying the camel's foreleg.*

*Page from Robert Graves book Lawrence and
the Arabs with annotation by Lawrence.*

*Talbot truck outside of Mudawara. The Talbots were used mostly to transport the 10 pd. mountain guns.
At Mudawara, Buxton used one to survey the station prior to the attack. Buxton is seated at the edge of the truck.*

Mudawara Station after its capture.

Watson and friends on the way to Mudawara, capturing the good humor and comradeship of the English soldier that Lawrence missed.

Siddons and his planes arrived and they dropped some bombs on the station. By seven in the morning, the last of the enemy surrendered. Twenty-one Turks were killed and one hundred and fifty prisoners taken. The English lost 4 killed and 11 wounded.

The Camel Corps demolished the station, arranged for some Arab troops to escort the prisoners to Akaba, and proceeded north to attack more railway lines. This second part of the campaign was soon called off when it was decided that further attacks on stations were not worth the risk of high casualties. The Turks had shifted more troops into the area.

Lawrence welcomed the men to Azrak and they were greeted with great celebration by Feisal at Aba el Lissan. Lawrence was extremely proud of the Camel Corps. He writes,

I told my men how from that three hundred I would pick forty fellows who would have out-ridden, out-fought and out suffered any forty Arabs in Feisal's army.

BUXTON'S MEN BLOWING UP MUDOWWARA STATION
Copyright

Page from Robert Graves book Lawrence and the Arabs.

Jambiya presented by Feisal to Buxton at Aba el Lissan. The stripes of the belt are representative of the Hejaz flag.

The Royal Navy and the Arab Revolt

An often-overlooked aspect of the Arab Revolt is the role the Royal Navy played in its success. From the beginning of the revolt in June 1916, the Royal Navy had control of the Red Sea. Rear Admiral Sir Rosslyn Wemyss was in charge of the naval operations in the Red Sea. He supervised the British patrols that kept the area clear of any Turkish gunboats. Assisting with this were three seaplane carriers. The use of seaplanes was just in its early stage. These planes were carried on board ship and placed on the sea with a crane for take off. They proved very useful for limited aerial reconnaissance and bombing.

When the Arabs attacked the Turkish-held seaport of Jidda in June 1916, British warships aided by shelling the town. Seaplanes assisted with bombing. After its capture, the Arabs continued their way northward attacking the coastal cities of Rabegh, Yenbo and Qunfidha. After capturing Yenbo, the port would be used to land weapons, ammunition and material. But by early December 1916, Turkish troops started to make a move on retaking it. Lawrence communicated with Captain W. E. Boyle, the Senior Naval Officer, Red Sea, the seriousness of the threatened attack and the need for naval assistance to help with its defense. In less than 24 hours, Boyle had five ships near Yenbo for its protection. A monitor, "M31", with a shallow

Admiral of the Fleet Sir Rosslyn Wemyss
At the start of the Arab Revolt, Vice Admiral Wemyss was Commander-in-Chief, East Indies and Egypt Station. He reorganized the Red Sea patrols and placed Captain Boyle in command. Lawrence gave Wemyss high praise for all his effort in the success of the Revolt.

Important notables at a planning meeting on board RIMS Dufferin, 1916. Back row, left to right includes Storrs, Cornwallis, Hogarth and Commander Warren, RN. Front row seated, left to right: Sherif Zeid, Sherif Shakir and Captain William Boyle RN.

H.M.S. Euryalus, for a time, the flagship of Wemyss. The Dufferin and the Euryalis guarded Akaba for weeks after its capture. Being a four-funnelled boat, Lawrence said it greatly impressed tribal opinion, since the more funnels, the greater the ship.

draft stayed close to the shore to cover any possible attack. Larger ships capable of firing shells over the town took up position. Defensive troop positions were made on land and through the night naval searchlights scanned the low flat plains. No attack came. Lawrence wrote:

> *Afterwards we heard the Turks' hearts had failed them at the silence and the blaze of lighted ships from end to end in the harbour, with the eerie beams of the searchlights revealing the bleakness of the glacis they would have to cross. So they turned back: and that night, I believe, they lost their war.*

With Yenbo now secured, Feisal's forces moved northward along the coast to Wejh. From Wejh, the forces could strike at the Hejaz Railway. The assault on Wejh

was to be a shared attack. A naval landing party with Arab troops would land north of the city and troops under Feisal would arrive from the south. The Arab army coming from the south fell way behind schedule and the attack was left for the troops from the north. Seaplanes spotted the firing of the naval guns of Hardinge and Fox. After 36 hours of fighting, the Turks surrendered Wejh and Feisal had the necessary coastal base to continue the revolt north.

In May, Lawrence and Nasir left Wejh to make their way to capture Akaba from the land. After its capture on July 6, Lawrence made his way to Suez personally. Allenby and Wemyss immediately sent the Dufferin loaded with food and stores. His flagship Euryalus arrived as well. This shifted the launch base for the

HMS Suva

Wonderful photograph of Snagge with an assortment of soldiers and sailors with British and Arab officers. Snagge holds the leash to his pet oryx, a gift from Feisal that became the ship's mascot.
In time, Snagge presented the oryx to the Cairo Zoo. Snagge, a career naval officer, stayed in touch with Lawrence, Feisal, Nuri and Jaafar after the war. He retired a Rear Admiral and died in 1955.

Captain Boyne RN with Zeid and Feisal, third and fourth from left, on board HMS Suva, 1916.
Lawrence appreciated the valuable support to the Arab Revolt provided by Boyle. Because of his red hair, the popular naval officer was called 'Ginger Boyle' by his men. A career sailor, he rose to the rank of Admiral of the Fleet.

A wounded and captured Jaafar Pasha with Captain Snagge of HMS Humber. Jaafar was captured during the Senussi Rebellion and imprisoned in Egypt. Later Jaafar would join the Arab Revolt and renew his friendship with Snagge.
His ship HMS Humber was guardship at Akaba.

revolt from Wejh to Akaba. Soon the monitor *Humber*, under the command of Captain Snagge, took up position as guard ship at Akaba. Snagge and his gunnery warrant officer assisted Lawrence in the technical use of electronic detonators for use against the nearby

The Ozarda and H.M.S. Hardinge off the coast of Akaba, late March 1918. Photo by Harry Chase.

The transport ship SS Ozarda. Men and supplies on board the Ozarda, March 1918, about to leave Egypt bound for Akaba. Passengers included Lowell Thomas, Harry Chase, and regular Hejaz and Egyptian troops. Photo by Harry Chase.

railway. Lawrence found Snagge's company and the comfort of his ship welcoming. *"His inquiring nature,"* Lawrence wrote,

> *took interest in the shore, and saw the comic side even in our petty disasters. To tell him the story of failure was to laugh at it, and for always a good story he gave me a hot bath, and tea with civilized trappings, free from every suspicion of blown sand. His kindness and help served us in lieu of visits to Egypt for repairs, and enabled us to hammer on against the Turks through month after month of feckless disappointment.*

Having complete and easy access by sea, the Arab Revolt could now be furnished with continuing supplies of food, guns, ammunition and gold. In *Seven Pillars* Lawrence gives gracious praise to the Royal Navy. He continues,

> *The Red Sea patrol-ships were the fairy godmothers of the Revolt. They carried our food, our arms, our ammunition, our stores, our animals. They built our piers, armed our defences, served as our coast artillery, lent us seaplanes, provided all our wireless communication, landed landing parties, mended and made everything. I couldn't spend the time writing down a tenth of their services.*

HMS Humber at Akaba. Lawrence and other officers found comfort in the ship's quarters and in Snagge's hospitality.

Bestowal document and notification of the award of the Turkish War Medal to a German soldier of the "Heeres Gruppen Kommando F" commanded by Liman von Sanders dated 25. 6 . 1918.

-The Ottoman Soldier-
Uniforms and equipment

There were approximately 20,000 Ottoman soldiers stationed in the Hejaz. German generals held overall command. General Erich von Falkenhayn held command of the army in Palestine until February 1918. He was succeeded by General Liman von Sanders, a veteran of the Gallipoli campaign, where he commanded the Turkish Fifth Army which was instrumental in stopping the Allied landings at Suvla Bay. As Commander-in-Chief, he would now lead the Turkish defense against Allenby and his advance in Palestine. Jemal Pasha, senior Ottoman commander, was the military governor of Syria and one of the leaders in the Turkish unsuccessful attack on the Suez Canal. He held command of the Ottoman Fourth Army. He made peace overtures to Feisal, which were rejected. Fakhri Pasha commanded the Twelve Army Corps at Medina. He led some expeditions out of the city to attack the Arabs, but for the most part stayed in Medina with 10000 troops. He held out until January 1919.

The Ottoman Army prior to World War One was retrained and organized by the Germans. Some of the Turkish officers went to Germany for additional training. Jaafar Pasha and Nuri as-Said were Arab officers in the Ottoman army.

The Cairo Intelligence Department produced an updated version of *The Handbook of the Turkish Army* in 1915. Primarily the work of Philip Graves, it also relied on the latest intelligence gathered from interviews of Turkish prisoners. The book contained 16 pages of Turkish army photographs and a colour chart showing the distinctive branches of the army. Lawrence helped with the printing of the book.

The Turkish soldier in the Hejaz wore a khaki tunic, more of a greenish brown than the sand colour khaki worn by the British troops. Matching trousers and puttees would also be worn. The headgear was uniquely Turkish. It looked like a kind of sun helmet but it was made by wound cloth over a wicker base. Called a *kabalak*, Enver Pasha is given credit with inventing it, earning the nickname, the *"enverie."* Officers usually wore a higher quality uniform, made of finer material. Their headdress was a lambskin wool cap, shaped like a fez, called a *kalpak*. In the Hejaz, many of the Arab Ottoman troops wore the traditional *keffiyeh*.

Turkish command staff wearing a variety of the Turkish headgear, the kabalak.

Turkish Order of the Medjidieh.
Established in 1852 by Sultan Abdul Mejid I.
This seven-pointed silver star has a gold center with the Sultan's tughra. The red enamel band around the center bears the words "Zeal, Devotion, Loyalty" and the year AH 1268 (1852) below.
During the First World War, this order was awarded to Turkish, German and Austrian soldiers.
Before the war, many British officers received the order for services for the Ottoman Empire, in the Crimea, Egypt and the Sudan.

Turkish Order of Osmanieh.
The Sultan Abdul Aziz established this order in 1862. The seven-pointed star in dark green enamel has a gold and red central medallion with a calligraphic inscription that reads, "Relying on the Assistance of Almighty God, Abdul Aziz Khan, Sovereign of the Ottoman Empire." The reverse has a trophy of arms and the year AH 699, the year of the founding of the Ottoman Empire. This was awarded to civil and military leaders for services to the state. Prior to World War I, a number of British officers received the award for work in Egypt and the Sudan.

Liyakat Medal.
This is the Turkish "Medal of Merit." A common military medal during the First World War, it was instituted in 1890. The obverse of the medal bears a trophy of arms with the sultan's cipher. The reverse reads "Medal of Merit for Those Who Have Shown Loyalty and Bravery," with the date AH 1308, the date of the founding of the medal. This example bears a ribbon clasp with crossed sabers with the year 1333 (1915). The medal was issued in gold and silver classes.

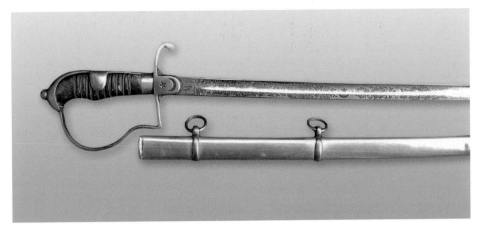

Turkish Infantry Officer's Sword. World War I period.
Patterned after the German infantry sword, the Turkish sword bears a star and crescent motif on the hilt and blade.

Boots and shoes were standard issue at the start of the war but footwear became a problem as the campaign progressed. Photographs of captured Turkish troops in 1918 show some wearing sandals and others with bare feet.

The equipment was mostly German-made. Most of the infantry was armed with the Mauser Model 1893 or 1903 rifle, though older model rifles were still in service. Six brown leather cartridge boxes were carried on a belt with a metal buckle bearing the star and crescent.

The Turkish Army had proved itself at Gallipoli. The British forces in general felt respect for *"Johnny Turk."* This started to change when reports of the Turkish abuse to the British prisoners taken at Kut became known.

In the Hejaz, some of the infantrymen's duties were long days stationed along the Hejaz Railway, protecting the line or helping with repairs. In Medina, once hemmed in by Abdulla and Ali, the troops just stayed on the defensive.

Lawrence was extremely critical of the Turkish Army and its leadership based on his first hand experiences of being captured at Deraa, witnessing the atrocities of the Turkish army at the village of Tafas, their not taking Arab prisoners, and the neglect of the Turkish wounded at the Damascus hospital. He had sympathy for the individual Turkish soldier but no respect for the officers, who he felt brought on this war by their own ambition.

Turkish army belt buckles, World War I period.
Two part, stamped brass buckle bearing a star and crescent design.
Brass buckle with applied silver star and crescent badge.
Officer's two part gilded brass buckle with star and crescent design and a crimson and gold belt.
Buckle top right: High ranking official's silver belt buckle with a wreath design forming a crescent with a star. This example was obtained by Bimbashi Garland.

Travelogue slide of Lowell Thomas and Lawrence at Aba el Lissan, 1918.
Thomas wears an American officer's uniform without rank or insignia.

-The Advance on Damascus-

By the time Lawrence returned to Akaba, major political agreements had been made public. After the Bolsheviks seized control in Russia, they released the texts of the major treaties of the Allied powers. The now public Sykes-Picot Agreement showed the post-war plans for the Middle East, the dividing up of the lands between France and Great Britain with no allowance of Arab aspirations. About the same time, the Balfour Declaration, calling for a Jewish homeland in Palestine was released. These agreements were in direct conflict with promises made to the Arabs. Lawrence felt he had led the Arabs on a lie, leading their fight for independence under false pretences. Lawrence seemed to resolve the conflicting promises by trying to play the Arabs' hand as strong as possible, putting them

in the best possible bargaining position once victory was achieved. He *"vowed to make the Arab Revolt the engine of its own success."* The Turks courted the Arab leaders with promises, pointing out how the British were betraying them. Lawrence was able to convince them that their best position was still with the British and Allenby.

Allenby was counting on strong Arab support east of the Dead Sea. To enable this, Allenby wanted the Arabs to form and maintain an army more in line with European traditions, in uniform and under orders. The Turkish-trained Jaafar Pasha worked on organizing the two thousand-man Regular Army, in British-provided uniforms and weapons.

Lawrence was forming up his own bodyguard. In part for his own need for personal safety and in the need

LAWRENCE AND HIS BODYGUARD AT AKABA
Summer, 1918
Copyright

Lawrence with some of his bodyguard at Akaba. Photograph annotated by Lawrence.

of having a small fighting force directly under his command, he recruited a group of ninety men, mostly Ageyli tribesmen. Lawrence paid them a wage of six pounds a month but provided their camels. Lawrence writes,

Fellows were very proud of being in my bodyguard, which developed a professionalism almost flamboyant. They dressed like a bed of tulips, in every colour but white; for that was my constant wear, and they did not wish to presume.

Lawrence says *"The British at Akaba called them cut-throats but they cut throats only to my order."* He armed half of them with Lewis or Hotchkiss machine guns, making them a mighty and mobile striking force. Carrying five days of flour in their saddlebags, they had a range of 200 miles between watering their camels.

To follow Allenby's plan, Feisal's army had to go north. The Turks had evacuated Aba el Lissan and Lawrence and his bodyguard moved there. Nasir and his force had cut the railway line. Sherif Zeid joined the Arab forces in the newly occupied village of Tafileh. Lawrence arrived and wanted the army to move further north. By January 25 the Turks launched a counter attack to take back Tafileh. Some estimated the Turkish army to be around one thousand men. Nasir and Lawrence organized the 600 men to defend the village. After initially fighting the Turkish advance, Lawrence pulled back the troops to a ridge on the southern edge.

Allenby by Francis Dodd.

Effectively using their artillery, the Arabs held line and went on an attack when additional Arab troops arrived to attack the Turkish right front. The Turkish army fled north in retreat. Turkish losses were 200 killed and 250 captured. The Arab army counted twenty-five killed and forty wounded.

Lawrence and bodyguard. Lawrence appears to be using a silver bowl and spoon from his silver canteen service made for him at Jidda.

Officier Hedjazien montant un dromadaire

Hejaz Camel Corps officer wearing British-supplied uniform and equipment. French postcard.

MOHAMMED EL DHEILAN FEISAL JAAFAR

AT GUWEIRA
Copyright French Army Photo. Dept.

Feisal and his staff at Guweira. An official French Army photographer Charles Winckelsen visited Feisal and his army in February 1918 and took a remarkable series of photographs. Lawrence annotated this copy that was printed in the Lawrence biography by Robert Graves.

*Inside Feisal's tent at Guweira. Seated next to Feisal is Jaafar Pasha.
Photograph by Charles Winckelsen.*

Lawrence was angry at the losses, thinking they were unnecessary. He felt they could have avoided the orthodox battle altogether and thus by avoiding any valued casualty, would have won. The battle also delayed the advance further north to Kerak. Bad weather now set in and more gold was needed to obtain support of the tribes and villages to the north.

Lawrence returned to the British base. The British staff and armoured cars were now north of Akaba at Guweira. Lieutenant-Colonel Alan Dawnay, Allenby's liaison officer to Feisal's army was there to see how the campaign was going. He was the perfect officer to understand the needs of the Hejaz force and obtain it. Lawrence thought he was Allenby's greatest gift to the revolt. The force at Akaba was now three thousand men, including a limited number of artillery, armoured cars, British and French mountain gun detachments and six planes of the Royal Flying Corps. Dawnay

Ronald Storrs, the Military Governor of Jerusalem, introduced Lowell Thomas to Lawrence. Storrs (right) with Brigadier-General A. B. Robertson on the balcony of Hotel Fast on the day Thomas met Lawrence. February 1918.

Auda's camp photographed by a member of the Imperial Camel Corps. A good shot of Auda's tent showing details of camel riding saddles, transport saddles and horse saddle trappings. A Hejaz flag can also be seen.

and the staff recognized the need of continued guerilla attacks along the railway with more responsibilities given to the regular army. The capture of Ma'an was singled out. Lawrence returned to Tafileh with 30000 pounds of gold for Zeid. While Lawrence headed north to look over the area around Karek, Zeid paid off the troops around Tafileh instead of using it to gain support with the nearby tribes and villagers. Lawrence blamed himself for the misuse of funds and the delay it would cause. He was disgusted and wanted out. It was up to Allenby again to convince Lawrence to stay. Allenby pointed out how essential the Arab support was needed on his eastern front. To help Lawrence with his transport problems, Allenby provided him with 700 camels. While at British headquarters in Jerusalem, Lawrence met the American reporter Lowell Thomas and his photographer Harry Chase. Lawrence extended an invitation to come out to Akaba.

Thomas and Chase arrived in Akaba on

Lawrence on the balcony of Hotel Fast, Jerusalem. February 1918. That day Lawrence invited Thomas and Chase to Arabia.

March 27th. Lawrence made arrangements for them to meet Arab leaders and other British officers. In several days they made their way sixty miles northeast to Aba el Lissan, where Lawrence and his bodyguard were camped. In Shobek, they photographed the regular Hejaz Army, worked their way to Petra and returned through Guweira photographing the armoured car and mountain battery crews. On April 10th, Thomas and Chase left Akaba with many notes and nearly two hundred photographs. This would provide the main portion of a travelogue that would make Lawrence a household name in post-war England.

At this time the British forces suffered a setback in taking Amman while the Arab forces were under pressure to capture Ma'an. Resisting the advice of Lawrence and Joyce, Jaafar al-Askari and Maulud el Mukhlus led their 4000-man regular army against the town. Initially they met with success but the town was strongly fortified with trenches and a secure garrison. After several days of fighting, the Arabs pulled back. The Turks were even able to get more troops from Amman to the town. Knowing any further direct attack would likely fail, the Arabs and British concentrated on destroying the rail around Ma'an, isolating the town. It would remain under siege until the end of the war.

The British armoured car units and mountain guns were used in many additional attacks along the railway, capturing stations, blowing up bridges and destroying track. Lawrence, Joyce, and Dawnay went on a number of these attacks, often accompanied by small numbers of Bedouin tribesmen, Arab regulars or Pisani and his mountain guns. A typical attack would signal out the targeted railway station, open the attack with gunfire from the armoured cars, call in the mountain guns for some well placed shell fire, leading to a final assault on

foot. In many cases, the Turks would have surrendered before the final assault.

Action on the Western Front now affected the plans in Palestine. A strong German offensive started in March and reinforcements were desperately needed. Allenby was having thousands of his regular troops pulled out and shipped to the front. Long-term plans called for these troops to be replaced by soldiers brought in mostly from India. Allenby needed several months for these troops to arrive and to be sufficiently trained. Any planned major offensive in Palestine would have to wait until September. This slow down also allowed the German and Turkish troops to build up their own defences.

Allenby was no longer in need of the Imperial Camel Corps, its troops sent back to their original units or posted to machine gun squadrons. Dawnay secured three hundred men of the Camel Corps to be loaned to Lawrence, leading to the capture of the station of Mudawara on August 8th and destroying bridges deep in the Turkish-held territory. The raid was a limited success, with the capture of the station and causing the Turks to fear a much larger British attack force coming from the south.

By September, Allenby's troops were ready to make their final push north to Damascus with Feisal, Lawrence and the Arab Northern Army leading the attack east of the Dead Sea. Making effective use of his cavalry, Allenby quickly advanced.

Lawrence gathered the armoured cars and troops north at Azrak to prepare for the attack on Deraa. The politics of the revolt threatened it again when Sherif Hussein suddenly fired the Hejaz commanders. Feisal himself threatened to

Maulud el Mukhlus, center, and some of his staff.

Lawrence at Akaba.

Lawrence with Winterton and Young. The tall and thin Winterton was a veteran officer of the Imperial Camel Corps and a member of the House of Commons. He joined Lawrence for the advance on Damascus. Hubert Young took over the difficult task of organizing supplies. Both men took part in raids on the railway and remained friends with Lawrence after the war.

walk away. Events were calmed down and the order restored with the help of faked telegrams from Hussein. By September 12th, the Arab and British forces were in place ready for the offensive. This included Nuri Said and Auda, Bedouin tribesmen and Arab regulars, Pisani and his gunners, the British armoured car units and mountain artillery, Peake and his Egyptian Camel Corps, Scott-Higgins and a small number of Ghurkas, Joyce, Stirling, Hubert Young and Earl Winterton, a diverse group and a who's who of personalities.

On September 14th, the force moved out for the Hejaz railway line and Deraa. Reaching the line Joyce and Lawrence destroyed a bridge, isolating Amman from Deraa. Peake and his Egyptians were madly destroying sections of track, planting hundreds of explosives. On the 17th, Lt. Junor, in his outdated BE 12 aircraft, attempted to fend off

The Sherif's Band. The band included some former members of a Turkish Army band so they could play many German and Turkish requests. The addition of bagpipes to the band may be traced to the small contingent of Scottish troops at Akaba. After the war, Peake incorporated bagpipes into the Arab Legion band and that tradition carries on today. The bass drummer, who rests his drum on a chair, appears to be using a drum that has been painted in the stripes of the Hejaz national flag.

German postcard showing Hejaz prisoners being escorted into Damascus.

attacking Turkish planes. He got them to flee but at the cost of his own aircraft. The now grounded pilot joined Lawrence's force. Lawrence and Young took a small group from the main force and moved north attacking the station at Mezerib and destroying more track and yet another bridge, the 79th, by Lawrence's count.

Lawrence made his way back to Azrak and was able to get a flight over to Allenby's headquarters to coordinate the plans for the final push on Damascus. Lawrence wanted more air support and fuel for the armoured cars. He also had the Arab forces gather at Um el Surab, to await the planes. On the 22nd, Lawrence arrived with three Bristol Fighters and a Handley Page bomber, loaded with needed supplies, causing tremendous excitement amongst the Arabs. Two days later, the Turkish army was retreating out of Amman and making their way north to Deraa. Feisal and Lawrence and the 4000 troops were ready to pursue them. As the Arab army split up to capture villages, little resistance was made. Hundreds of Turks were surrendering. A retreating Turkish column leaving Deraa passed through the village of Tafas killing many civilians. When the Arab army entered the village and saw the atrocities, they attacked the retreating Turkish army and showed no mercy. Lawrence gave an order of no prisoners. Intervention by some of the British officers prevented the entire Turkish detachment from being massacred. The Arabs captured the main railway station at Deraa on September 28th. General Barrow and a group of British cavalry arrived to witness the Arabs pillaging the town and stripping the wounded Turks. Getting no help from Lawrence to restore order, Barrow ordered his men to put it to a stop. By now the Turkish army was in full retreat and were surrendering by

the thousands. A column of Turks were trapped in a valley and subjected to intense aerial bombing by the British. With Allenby's army steadily advancing to the north and western edge of Damascus, the Arabs were coming from the south and eastern side. By September 30th, the armies were on the outskirts of the city.

The British staff at Akaba had a number of pets including several salukis. This little monkey, usually tethered to a pole, was nick-named "the Akaba ape."

*Lawrence's small gold jambiya in the collection
of All Souls College, Oxford.*

-Lawrence's Weapons and Arab Clothing-

Lawrence took great pride in being a good shot. He most likely had his first experiences with shooting from his father who was an enthusiastic sportsman. While a student at Oxford University, Lawrence was a member of the Oxford Officers Training Corps and became very good at shooting a pistol.

When he travelled to explore the Crusader Castles of Syria in 1909, he carried a Mauser model 1896 semi-automatic pistol. This expensive gun had the advantage of carrying ten high-velocity cartridges. One of its more famous users was Winston Churchill. He used this weapon quite effectively during the cavalry charge at Omdurman. In October 1909, Lawrence wrote his mother telling her that he

sold my Mauser pistol (at a profit) in Beyrout on my departure (5 pounds)

Returning to the Middle East in 1911, he again used firearms. In his letters home he mentions spending some free time target shooting and doing some hunting. He used a Mannlicher-Schoenauer carbine that he likely received as a gift. This was a fine target rifle and Lawrence became very proficient in using it. He mentions hitting a six-gallon petrol tin four out of five shots. Even more impressive, he states he hit an orange crate five out of five shots at 500 yards and nailed a meter square target three out of ten shots at 1,200 yards. He also mentions pistol shooting. A photograph taken by Lawrence of his friend Dahoum shows him holding a Colt automatic pistol; most likely it is Lawrence's pistol. Lawrence was also quite proud of his shooting with the pistol. He writes of hitting a Turkish coin five times out of seven shots at 25 yards while rapid firing the Colt Automatic. On a more practical level, he writes about pistol shooting two ducks for his dinner guests, hitting them in the head at twenty yards.

When the war started, Lawrence was able to obtain two Colt Automatic .45 caliber Model 1911 pistols from the United States, purchased by a friend who was travelling there. He sent one to his brother Frank, who was an officer in the Gloucestershire Regiment. Frank shared his

Lawrence's rifle showing the Turkish presentation inscription and his own carved initials and date.

Photo of Dahoum with Lawrence's Colt automatic pistol.

Lawrence also used a Short Model Lee-Enfield. He provided a history of this rifle in a letter written to his friend E. T. Leeds. He informs Leeds he will present his rifle to Charles ffoulkes, curator of the Tower and collecting artifacts for what would become the Imperial War Museum. Lawrence writes,

> I've got a trophy he would like for his War Museum. The Turks took four of the short Lee-Enfield rifles taken at Gallipoli, and engraved them in gold on the chamber 'Part of our booty in the battles for the Dardanelles' in the most beautiful Turkish script. Deeply cut by hand, and then gold wire beaten in. Four of the rifles were sent, one to each of the sons of the Sherif of Mecca. I carry Feisul's, which he gave me (it's a 1st Essex gun) and I'm trying to get Zeid's, which I'll send C.J.ff. if I win. They form admirable gifts, tell him. Ali has one, but Abdullah's has been given to Ronald Storrs, the oriental secretary to the Residency here.

This rifle is inscribed above the magazine "T. E. L. 4.12.16" It also has five notches carved in the stock, representing the Turks shot by Lawrence. After the war Lawrence presented this rifle to King George V, who in turn presented it to the Imperial War Museum where it is almost always on display.

In the Hejaz, Lawrence also carried a Lewis Gun. This was most unusual but Lawrence was always willing to take advantage of any technological advancement. He carried a stripped down version, stored in a long leather bucket in his camel saddlebag. This machine gun used heavy round magazines that fitted over the barrel, holding 47 or 97 rounds. Lawrence also obtained some Lewis Guns for his bodyguard to use. On the Western Front, the Lewis Gun was typically used by a two-man crew, set on the ground, using a bipod.

interest in shooting and when he had the pistol in hand, taking it apart challenged him, but he was soon the envy of his fellow officers who had the lesser Webley pistols. Frank located a supplier of Colt parts and ammunition in London and offered to get Lawrence anything he might need. The Colt pistol seemed to be carried by Lawrence during the Hejaz campaign. There is a photograph of him taken during an expedition with George Lloyd where he appears to be cocking the Colt pistol.

Camels with several saddles having a Lee-Enfield slung over the back pommel.

Lt. Wood, Royal Engineers, on the left, holding a Lee-Enfield Mk III, similar to the rifle used by Lawrence.
On the right, Lawrence holding a Colt automatic pistol. Photograph by George Lloyd.

Lawrence did keep a Webley revolver at his Clouds Hill cottage and recent excavations of a tree on the grounds recovered some bullets from its trunk.

Arab clothing

If you wear Arab things, wear the best. Clothes are significant amongst the tribes, and you must wear the appropriate, and appear at ease in them. Dress like a Sherif, if they agree to it.

This was Lawrence's advice to British officers serving with the Arabs. He adds in *Seven Pillars of Wisdom* that

The army uniform was abominable when camel riding or when sitting on the ground; and Arab things, which I learned to manage before the war, were cleaner and more decent in the desert.

These "*Arab things*" were simple, practical items of clothing for working in the desert. They primarily consisted of a *thob*, *zebun*, *abayeh*, *keffiyeh* and *agal*.

The *thob* is a simple white garment, similar to an ankle length shirt, with long sleeves and a collar. Some variations on sleeve design and decorative embroidery can be found. The *thob* most often would be bound at the waist, from a simple plain rope up to a decorative belt depending on the taste and status of the wearer.

In this photograph, Lawrence wears the smaller, gold jambiya made to his specifications in Mecca. 1918.

An agal belonging to Lawrence. This agal was left with the artist Stuart Reid. This variation of agal is attached at the corners. This agal and an abayeh belonging to Lawrence, also left with Reid, are in the collection of the Australian War Memorial. Other Lawrence agals are in the collections of All Souls College and the Imperial War Museum. An agal given by Clare Sydney Smith by Lawrence is in a private collection.

Wade's agal unwound.

An abayeh given by Lawrence to his friend Vyvyan Richards. This example is unusual in that it is sleeved. Most abayehs were not.

Over this robe, a *zebun* could be worn. Some examples of this type of cloak are richly embroidered or made of fine silk. They are cut like a western style, ankle length bathrobe.

The most common everyday outer garment is the *abayeh*. This wide, sleeveless cloak is commonly made of woven camel hair, cotton or silk with metallic woven embroidery stitched around the neck and down a portion of the sides. Lawrence wrote home from Akaba:

Do you remember a very light dusty-amber silk cloak I brought back with me once from Aleppo? If it is not in use, I would be very glad to have it sent to me. Arab clothes are hard to find, now-a-days with manufacture and transport thrown out of gear.

Lawrence would wear a *keffiyeh* headcloth held in place by an *agal*. The keffeyah would be a solid or patterned piece of cloth about a meter or larger square. This would

Thob belonging to Lawrence. This robe is likely the same garment worn in the Harry Chase photographs of Lawrence taken in London. This long hanging sleeved example is less common. Most thobs are of the "shirt sleeve" variety.

Lawrence's brown and white striped silk abayeh
and thob displayed at the Imperial War Museum.

White and gold silk abayeh with embroidered decoration.
Feisal presented this garment to Lawrence. This type of garment
would have been worn on only special occasions.

Agal and keffiyeh worn by Lt. E. H. Wade of the Hejaz Armoured Car Battery. Lawrence provided headdress for the officers and men of
the Hejaz Armoured Car Battery.

This photograph of Lawrence was taken by Harry Chase at the Hotel Fast in Jerusalem, 1918. It shows Lawrence wearing his second dagger, a gift from Sherif Nasir. After the war, Lawrence left this dagger with the artist Kathleen Scott, while posing for a sculpture.

be folded in half at the corners making a triangle. Early in the campaign, Lawrence wrote home:

If that silk headcloth with the silver ducks on it…still exists, will you send it out to me?

Holding down the *keffiyeh* would be the *agal*. The *agal* could be a simple woven goat hair rope doubled over. Men of higher status would wear an *agal* woven with metallic thread and silk with a hanging tassel or two hanging down the back. British soldiers of the armoured car units wore the Arab headdress and not surprisingly, only the officers wore the fancier *agals*.

Around the waist, most Bedouin wore a dagger called a *jambiya*. These also were highly prized and varied in quality. There were also differences in style determined by the region the wearer came from. No matter how ornate the dagger might be, in almost all cases, the blade itself was poorly made.

Lawrence had three daggers. His first dagger was given to him by Sherif Abdulla. He wore it during the trek to capture Akaba until Sherif Nasir, the leader of the expedition, collected the better daggers of his men and presented them as gifts to the Howeitat chiefs. His second dagger was of a different style, an Indo Persian design, presented to him by Sherif Nasir. Lawrence wore this silver gilt dagger around Akaba. He adds:

It was a heavy thing and I discarded it with pleasure for the gold one which had been made small by my order: and the gold one I wore for the rest of the war, except when it was being repaired or re-belted."

After the war, Lawrence had this dagger valued by Spinks at 125 pounds. He sold it to his friend Lionel Curtis. He later presented it to All Souls College where it is today.

George Lloyd's aide Thorne, photographed at Guweira, wearing a striped abayeh and using a typical saddlebag.

Nesib el Bekr wearing typical Arab clothing, on a camel with high quality saddlebags. These colorfully woven, tasseled saddlebags are similar to the fine quality camel accoutrements that Lawrence used.

Lawrence wears his first dagger, a larger style jambiya. This was presented to him by Sherif Abdulla. Taken at Rabegh aerodrome, March 1917.

In this photograph, Lawrence wears the smaller, gold jambiya made to his specifications in Mecca. 1918.

Lawrence in front of his tent at Akaba. Lawrence wears a decorative woven paisley cloth zebun, over his thob. After the war, Lawrence modified a very similar zebun into a dressing gown. His brother M. R. Lawrence later presented this zebun to the Museum of Costume at Bath. Around his waist, Lawrence wears his larger silver gilt jambiya. His Bedouin type camel saddle can be seen on the right.

Mahmas, a camel driver who worked with Lawrence's bodyguard, photographed by Lawrence.

-Lawrence as Photographer-

Lawrence got his interest in photography from his father Thomas Lawrence, an avid amateur photographer. We can speculate that Thomas took some of his family's group photographs since he does not appear in any of them. Arnold Lawrence, T. E.'s younger brother, presented two cameras to the Museum of the History of Science, Oxford. One of these cameras belonged to his father; the other was made for and used by T. E. Lawrence.

His father's camera is a half-plate field camera made by 'R & J Beck of London.' Arnold notes that his father was using this camera by 1890. Included with this camera is an additional lens made by Taylor and Hobson, purchased by Thomas Lawrence to take long distance shots. There are no known collections of his photographs in any institution so we cannot judge his proficiency and skill as a photographer. There are, however many photographs taken by his son.

The earliest identified photograph taken by T.E. is a group photograph of students of the VI Form, City of Ox-ford High School. T. E. is standing off to the right with bulb in hand snapping the photograph. His classmate T. O. Balk remembers the photograph being taken in July 1907 on the lawn in front of the school. "*Ned Lawrence was the prime mover in making the record of a very pleasant year. He persuaded the Head to give his consent and also the time needed to arrange the group and photograph it.*" He used his own camera, set on a tripod, connected by a rubber tube and a bicycle pump. Lawrence made prints for everyone in the group.

On his first trip to France to explore castles, Lawrence did not bring a camera. He was too concerned about the space it would take up. He wrote to his mother in 1906 about the castle at Fougeres,

Inside the castle is all destroyed; it is but a shell though a glorious one… I shall certainly return next year for another examination, and I shall bring a camera with me: Father's one if possible: it is a paradise for a photographer.

One of a number of Lawrence's photographs of Feisal's army on the move.

Lawrence the ability to take close up or long distance shots with the shutter speed allowing exposures for almost any type of lighting conditions.

While at Carchemish, Lawrence dutifully recorded the archeological finds with this camera or one of three others that were at the site. By his count, he took over two hundred photographs during the 1911 season. Lawrence had expanded his subjects to include friends and locals as well. We can see him taking portraits of workers, their villages and always more landscapes. He even records interior shots of the group's living quarters. Lawrence takes on the job of documenting the 'experience' of Carchemish, going beyond just taking photos of found objects.

Lawrence and Woolley were the appointed archeologists with Newcombe's mapping team in the Wilderness of Zin. Lawrence was the main photographer for the expedition. The original photographs and negatives are in the collection of The Palestine Exploration Fund, in London. Recent research by Dr. Rubert Chapman and Shimon Gibson has determined which of the photographs were taken by Woolley or Lawrence. It was determined that photographs with the nitrate film negatives were taken by Woolley. Photographs with glass plate negatives were taken by Lawrence.

By the start of the war, photography was growing in popularity and reasonable in price. Kodak was making smaller cameras with rolled film. Major cities had processing labs available. It was advertised for its ease and affordability. Many officers took cameras with them to the front. Documenting the war would become a much more personal, individual remembrance.

Lawrence seems to have taken no photographs while in Egypt, in contrast to his fellow officers who took many snaps of the local Egyptians, the many monuments, ruins or mosques. Lawrence brings a camera to the Hejaz though. It seems early on that the Arab Bureau officials, and perhaps even Lawrence, recognized the importance of the Arab Revolt to be documented. Lawrence starts to record the cities of Yenbo, Jidda and Wejh. He records his visits into the desert, the oasis, and landscapes. Individual portraits are taken as well. Lawrence takes a remarkable series of photographs of Feisal's army on the march. He records his view in an unusual panoramic sort of way. Riding a camel toward the front

On the return trip to France in the summer of 1907, he did bring a camera. When we look at his photographs from that trip, many of them are documentary photographs, recording specific aspects of castles and their details. However, he shows a good eye for composition too. In addition to the needed shots of castles, he also records the landscape of the area. He shoots Mont St. Michel with a telephoto lens 15 miles away capturing a cloudy atmosphere with a silhouetted foreground. He takes pictures of parts of castles shot through an open window, used as a frame. He puts trees in parts of the foreground to add depth to his image. He photographs church sculptures with an awareness of light and shadow. He knows how to line up a good shot and displays an artistic awareness of capturing that image.

Lawrence brought a camera with him for his 1909 walking tour of Syria. Though he was able to take some photographs, his camera was stolen while a watchman slept.

By early 1910, Lawrence was helping his friend, E. T. Leeds of the Ashmoleon Museum, by taking photographs and making lantern slides of medieval pottery in the collection. That summer Lawrence graduated with a First in Modern History from Jesus College. In the fall, he accepted a position to work at Carchemish with D. G. Hogarth. Part of his duties would be to photograph their archeological finds. He had a camera built to his specifications. He would use it for the next four years. This is the second camera in The Museum of the History of Science collection.

This Lawrence camera is thought to have been made by J. H. Dallmeyer of London. It is a front focusing camera with specific modifications to help with architectural photography. It has a shutter speed from 1 to 1/250 of a second. It includes five lenses including a telephoto lens and a wide angle one. There are provisions for taking eight glass slides. The camera and accessories fit into a leather box with a printed inscription reading '*Property of T. E. Lawrence, Pole Hill, Chingford, Essex*'. When Lawrence ordered this camera, he certainly knew the results he wanted to get from it. This camera is way beyond what an amateur photographer would need. This camera gave

Photograph of Azrak from Robert Graves book with notations by Lawrence stating this photo was taken after the Cairo Conference, 1921.

Photograph of Azrak from Robert Graves book with notations by Lawrence stating this photo was taken after the Cairo Conference, 1921.

of the group, near Feisal, Lawrence points his camera to the side and starts taking pictures, again and again. He captures the army on the move. Commenting on this series of photos, Lawrence says they were taken from the saddle while riding in Wadi Yenbo and that it *"would take a great painter, of course, to do justice to the astonishing life and movement of the Bedouin armies, because half the virtue of them lies in the colours of the clothes and saddle trappings."* Within the limits of black and white, Lawrence captures it quite well.

In February 1917, Lawrence writes his family;

I hope to be able to send you some photographs of the Sherif and of Feisul and the rest of us shortly.

Towards the end of the month Lawrence is back in Cairo and able to get his film processed.

I enclose a few photographs-as long as they are not published there is no harm in showing them to anyone. I have a lot more, but they have not been printed yet. They will give you an idea of the sort of country (in the oases) and the sort of people we have had to do with. It is of course by far the most wonderful time I have had.

Lawrence knows in many cases he is just documenting the landscape, the desert mountains and wide barren plains. He also tries to capture a sense of the atmosphere of being on campaign. He recognizes that sometimes he just gets it right. In a letter home from Akaba January 1917 he singles out a particular photograph that the Arab Bureau hopes to publish in the *Illustrated London News.*

One of the prints to appear, showing the Sherifian camp at dawn, in Wadi Yenbo, was taken by me at 6 a.m. in January last, and is a very beautiful picture. Most sunrise pictures are taken in sunset, but this one is really a success.

In addition to the motion shots taken on camel back of Feisal's army, there are a number showing Feisal's army coming into Wejh, dwarfed by the landscape. The Hejaz photos of Lawrence not only document the landscape but also include many shots of the personalities of the revolt itself. He photographs Auda, Sherif Shakir and Sherif Nasir. He is able to record the march to Akaba, culminating with the now iconic shot of the Arab

standard bearer advancing in the midst of a sandstorm.

Lawrence seems to have taken few photos in the Hejaz after the spring of 1918. By that time he had taken over two hundred photographs. For the rest of the campaign, the photographic record is provided by others. The French send two cameramen to the Hejaz and take photographs of primarily the French soldiers in the area but also do local natives and leading Arab figures. Lawrence is in Akaba when Lowell Thomas and Harry Chase arrive. He sits for a number of shots and would have been curious about Chase's still and motion picture cameras. Some of Lawrence's fellow officers had cameras and we have numerous shots taken by Goslett and Ramsey. Douglas Peerman of the Imperial Camel Corps documented the entire Mudawara operation. After the war, Lawrence was able to put many of his photographs, and others given to him, in a scrapbook. Some of these entire pages are preserved in the Imperial War Museum and the Bodleian Library. Lawrence actively sought photos from others to supplement his own collection of Hejaz photos. He loaned some of his photos to artists while working on illustrations for *Seven Pillars of Wisdom* and some of these are obvious inspirations for several of the works of William Roberts. Lawrence also provided some of his own photographs to Lowell Thomas for his print articles. He loaned others to Robert Graves and Liddell Hart for their biographies.

Lawrence took few photographs after the war. He did take some photographs of Jidda when he returned in 1921. While in the Royal Air Force, he attended a photography class at Farnborough. Though it seems he was no longer an active photographer, he did allow himself to be a willing subject of some notable photographic sessions, by Harry Chase in London in 1919, Flight Lieutenant Smetham in Miranshah 1928, Howard Coster in London 1931, and his friend Wing Commander Reginald Sims, in February 1935.

Lawrence assembled a photographic scrapbook of the Hejaz campaign including photographs sent to him from fellow officers. The notations are his. The Q numbers are the Imperial War Museum photo numbers written by staff. Some of these rare scrapbook pages are in the collections of the Imperial War Museum and the Bodleian Library.

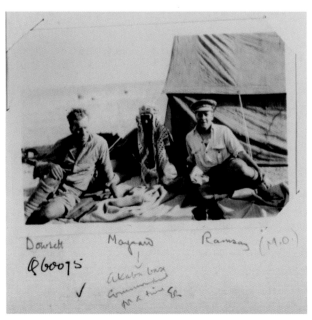

9b0096. George Lloyd, TEZ, Ahmed, Abd el Rahman at Batra. (G.LL photo)

9b0094. In Wadi Itm. (G.LL photo)

Scrapbook Page

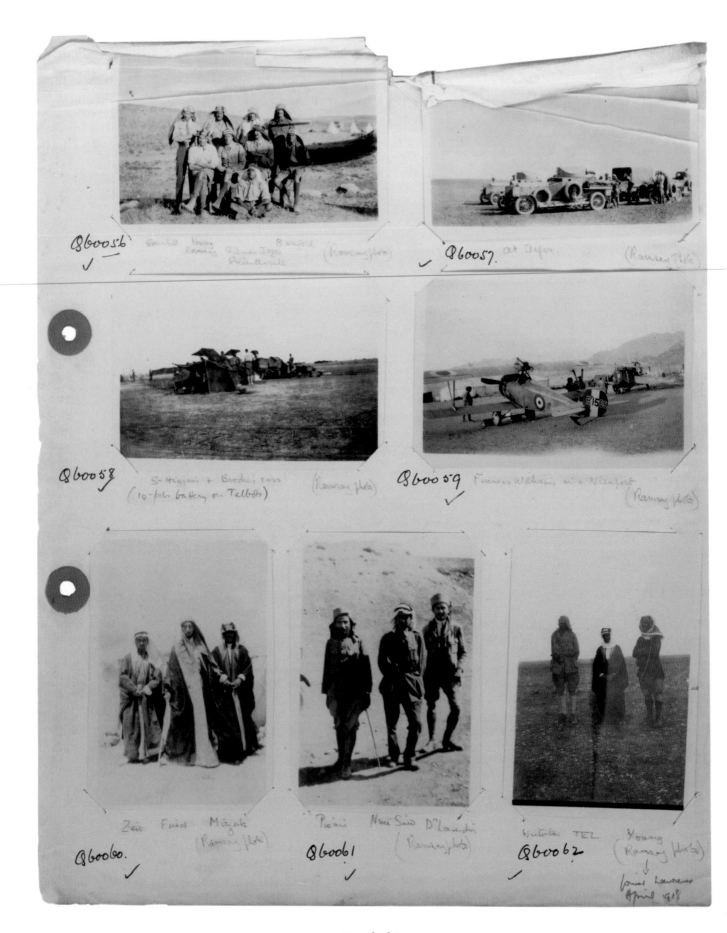

Scrapbook Page

Scrapbook Page

LAWRENCE AT ~~VERSAILLES~~
Copyright Damascus 2·X·18
taken by Colonel Findlay, American army.

Photograph of Lawrence at Damascus from the Robert Graves biography,
corrected and annotated by Lawrence for Sydney Smith.

-Damascus-

At dawn on October 1st, Lawrence and Stirling, in the Rolls Royce tender *Blue Mist*, were heading toward Damascus. The night before the Turks decided to evacuate the city, turning it over to a provisional government. Allenby made it clear to his corps commanders not to enter the city, unless forced to for tactical reasons.

Allenby recognized the importance for Damascus to be liberated by the Arabs with their provisional government running it. As Commander-in-Chief of all operations, Allenby would still be in overall command.

Lawrence and Stirling were delayed briefly when freshening up by a stream they were temporarily "captured" by some Indian lancers. After some delay, the British officer in charge released them. By 9 a.m., they were entering Damascus. The night before, several thousand Rualla horsemen had entered the city, preparing the city with news of the coming Arab forces. Hours before Lawrence, men of the 3rd Light Horse Brigade were welcomed with great joy. About that same time Sherif Nasir and Nuri Shaalan were arriving in the southern edge of the city. The streets were filled with a welcoming population. Lawrence said the crowds:

> yelled themselves hoarse, danced, cut themselves with swords and daggers and fired volleys in the air. Nasir, Nuri Shaalan, Auda abu Tayi and myself were cheered by name, covered with flowers, kissed indefinitely and splashed with attar of roses from the house tops.

By October 2nd, General Chauvel and his Desert Mounted Corps officially entered the city. Much of the city was still in disarray, with wounded Turks uncared for

Lawrence in his Rolls Royce tender Blue Mist. Damascus. October 1918. Lawrence's right hand is bandaged. The driver wears a keffiyeh and simple agal over his army service cap.

Egyptian newspaper announcing the capture of Damascus by the Arab and Allied armies.

On October 3rd Allenby and his staff entered the city. He had received his orders from the War Office on how to proceed politically, stressing the enforcement of the Anglo-French agreements and limiting where the Arab lands would be, essentially from Akaba to Damascus,

and a general lack of water and food. Lawrence was doing his best to get the city under control. Lawrence headed to the Town Hall and found out that the provisional government was already being challenged. A group led by the alleged traitor Abd el Kader and his brother was taking charge. Lawrence had them forcefully removed and established an Arab administration under Feisal's pick, Shukri, as military governor. Martial law was proclaimed, police guards posted and looting brought under control. The government dealt with getting power back up, sanitation under control, a fire brigade organized, relief work started, the railway back in service and the telegraph repaired. General Chauvel headed to the Town Hall to met Lawrence to see what order was being enforced. There was disagreement between the two on how Damascus would be controlled. Chauvel finally agreed to the Arab administration pending further word from Allenby. Lawrence recognized he needed Allenby's troops to help maintain order.

The "Blue Mist" surrounded by curious British soldiers immediately after Lawrence left it. A note on their copy of this photograph at the Imperial War Museum records that Captain Goslett of the Hejaz Armoured Car Ompany identified the driver as Corporal McKechnie of the Army Service Corps. At times this driver has been misidentified as S. C. Rolls or even Major Stirling.

east of the Jordan River. Britain would have a mandate over Palestine and France would control Lebanon with a protectorate over Syria.

That day, Feisal arrived in Damascus by train from Deraa and went escorted by his troops to meet with Allenby. Lawrence would translate for Feisal.

Allenby welcomed Feisal, his ally in arms, who was quite emotional from the great welcome he had received from the people of Damascus. Feisal thanked Allenby for his trust in

him and the Arab movement. Allenby explained to Feisal the limits that would be imposed on his Arab government and the division of the lands between British and French influence. According the Chauvel's notes on this meeting, Feisal acted surprised at the French involvement and believed that any land settlement would include Syria and Lebanon for the Arabs. When Allenby challenged Lawrence about his knowledge of the French involvement, Lawrence claimed he did not know of it. Finally Allenby reminded

Feisal and Allenby in Syria, 1919.

Feisal that he, Allenby, was Commander-in-Chief and that he, Feisal, was at the moment a Lieutenant-General under his command and under his orders. When the meeting was over and Feisal had left the Victoria Hotel, Lawrence asked Allenby if he could take leave, return to England, his task being finished. The next day, Lawrence left Damascus.

Arriving in the *Blue Mist*, on the outskirts of the city, Lawrence stopped to say farewell to Peake. He and his camel corps were readying supplies to move out. Lawrence asked Peake for the small railway station bell they had taken during the raid on Deraa. Peake gave it to him for he certainly felt Lawrence deserved it more than he

did. The bell joined a number of small souvenirs brought home by Lawrence. When he got to Cairo, Lawrence wrote an article for *The Times* detailing the capture of Damascus and the latest events of the Arab Revolt. It was time to put the cause for Arab independence out to the public. Lawrence was determined to work the political and public stages to win support for Feisal's case and prevent the French from taking Syria.

Lawrence was back in England by the last week of October and went to visit his family in Oxford. He quickly started making calls on influential politicians privately and started to appear before their committees. He was pushing to see the Sykes-Picot Agreement tossed out or greatly modified. He lobbied for the Arab claim of land and independence. Lawrence made suggestions on new national borders, allowing for spheres of influence and kingdoms for the sons of Hussein. Scheduled in between these many meetings, Lawrence had a private audience with King George V at Buckingham Palace. The purpose was for the King to present to Lawrence the actual awards of the Companion of the Bath and the Distinguished Service Order, granted to Lawrence for his gallantry during the Arab Revolt. Lawrence refused to accept the honours, making his case for the Arab cause to the King. He felt he could not accept honours from the British Government that was breaking its word to the Arabs. The King seemed to take this all in stride but some government officials viewed Lawrence's action with anger. You simply did not embarrass the King. When the story did get out, it did draw attention to how strongly Lawrence felt about the Arab cause. Continued days of lobbying led up to Armistice Day. On that evening of November 11th, Lawrence, his long time friend E. T. Leeds, and Charles ffoulkes, head of the new Imperial War Museum and medieval arms enthusiast, gathered for a quiet dinner overlooking Trafalgar Square, filled with a cheering population. The push for Arab independence would shift to a more prominent stage, the conference at Versailles.

Beautiful examples of "trench art" commemorating the liberation of Damascus. The brass artillery shells have been decorated by highly skilled Syrian craftsmen, incised and inlaid with silver and copper.

Damascus town square. Lawrence's "Blue Mist" can be seen in front of the lorries on the far right.

Formal photograph of Lawrence taken in Paris at the time of the Peace Conference. Lawrence wore a British officer's tunic with the rank of Colonel but with no ribbons of the orders and medals that he was entitled to wear. As a member of Emir Feisal's delegation, he would wear the agal and keffiyeh.

-Versailles Peace Conference-

In November 1918, Lawrence wrote to Hussein asking him to appoint Feisal to be his representative at the Peace Conference. It was clear that the best possibility of achieving Arab goals now laid at a bigger stage. At Versailles would be representatives of the Allied governments, including Woodrow Wilson who made clear his position of local populations having self-determination to settle their own future. French and British politicians were already pushing their wants. The French were demanding Syria. The British were wanting to keep Mesopotamia, knowing that its fields could provide needed grain for India and its oil, making Britain less dependent on other foreign sources. Both governments saw the advantage of reaching an understanding before the Americans became involved.

Feisal arrived in France in late November. The French would only recognize him as a military leader, not a negotiator for his father's cause. It was becoming obvious that the push would be for the enforcement of the Sykes-Picot Treaty. Lloyd George and Clemenceau reached an agreement giving Britain control of Palestine and Mesopotamia and the French getting greater Syria. Lawrence met up with Feisal and they made their way to England wanting to strengthen their position, still thinking they could pressure the British government to scrap the Sykes-Picot Agreement. In meetings with the British leaders, it became obvious to Lawrence that the British would rather anger the Arabs than anger the French. If Feisal wanted to lobby for his position, he was welcome to do it on his own and seek American sympathy. Feisal and Lawrence met with Chaim Weizmann. Feisal was willing to accept a Zionist population in Palestine for financial support toward his goal in Syria. While in London, Feisal went to an audience with King George V to be presented with the Royal Victorian Order, with Lawrence acting as interpreter. It was just weeks after Lawrence turned down his own honours from the King.

The Peace Conference was underway in January 1919. Lawrence would serve as an official advisor to Feisal. Despite French protests, Feisal would be able to represent his father and present their views at the conference. Feisal, in full Arab regalia and Lawrence, in British khaki officers uniform and Arab headdress quickly attracted the attention of the press. They met with the American delegation that they found were very sympathetic to their call for an independent Arab nation. When the Americans pressed for an independent commission to go to Syria and get the will of the people, the French reacted strongly in opposing it. They also suggested it if that be the case, send a commission to Mesopotamia as well, thus undermining the British ambitions in that area. Feisal's talk of a Pan-Arab union was overly ambitious and not well received, even by British moderates.

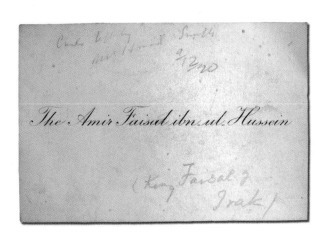

Card given by Feisal during his visit to England, 1919.
During his visit, he had an audience with King George V, met Lloyd George, attended the presentation of the
Freedom of the City of London to General Allenby and saw a performance of the Lowell Thomas travelogue.

Press photograph of Feisal and his aides.

Lawrence downplayed the idea, realizing how unworkable that was and pushed instead for small independent states.

By mid-April with the conference winding down, hope of an independent Arab state in Syria was over. Clemenceau met with Feisal and said the French would only be willing to work with Feisal, but they would be in charge of Syria. Feisal left for Damascus to await the arrival of the Commission, his last hope of undermining the French. Lawrence called the months of Paris the worst he had lived through.

Lawrence would continue his effort for the Arab cause. In letters to the press, he pointed out the weaknesses of current British policy. He used his growing popularity as a public war hero, brought on by Lowell Thomas, to freely push his ideas for settling the Middle East. By August 1920, the French forced Feisal out of Syria. In a letter to *The Times*, Lawrence wrote,

The Arabs rebelled against the Turks during the war not because the Turk government was notably bad, but because they wanted independence. They did not risk their lives in battle to change masters, to become British or French citizens, but to win a show of their own.

By February 1921, Lawrence joined the Middle East Department of the Colonial Office working for Winston Churchill. He would once again have a chance to push his views for the area.

Signed photograph of Feisal's minister Nuri Said. He wears the Hejaz officer's uniform patterned after the British uniform. His medal ribbons include the British Military Cross.

In March 1921, Churchill gathered 40 leading experts of the Middle East to meet at the Cairo Conference. Lawrence would work with war colleagues Hubert Young and Jaafar Pasha. Gertrude Bell, Arnold Wilson and Kinahan Cornwallis presented strong opinions about Iraq. The agreements reached put Feisal on the throne of Iraq and his brother Emir Abdullah in charge of Transjordan. Lawrence finally felt some justice was arrived at by giving thrones to two sons of the King of the Hejaz. Hussein did not take this arrangement well. Lawrence went to Jidda and appealed to him to endorse the plan, but he firmly refused to. He felt this was still a betrayal to Arab independence. By 1924, Hussein would be forced to abdicate, leaving Hejaz, that area firmly in control of Ibn Saud. Feisal ruled Iraq until his death in 1933. His grandson King Feisal II was murdered during a coup in 1958. Abdullah became King of Jordan in 1946 and was assassinated in 1948. His great grandson Abdullah is the current King of Jordan succeeding his father Hussein in 1999. Writing to Robert Graves, Lawrence viewed the Cairo Conference results *"the big achievement of my life: of which the war was a preparation."*

Press photograph of Lawrence used when announcing his participation at the Cairo Conference.

Revealing portrait of Thomas taken while in Arabia, printed from a broken glass plate negative.

-Lowell Thomas Travelogue-

He has invented some silly phantom thing, a sort of matinee idol in fancy dress, that does silly things and is dubbed "romantic."

T. E. *Lawrence to E. S. Greenhill,*
March 20, 1920

Lawrence was writing about Lowell Thomas. By the spring of 1920 over one million people had attended the Thomas travelogue *With Allenby in Palestine and Lawrence in Arabia*. Using motion picture film and hand colored slides taken by his accomplished photographer Harry Chase, Thomas presented an enthusiastic narration to a colorful account of the recent campaign. The audience was taken in by the multi media presentation. The reviews were ecstatic. Lawrence attended the show several times and made arrangements for his mother and brother Arnold to see it. Lowell Thomas had made Lawrence into a romantic war hero, the gallant English archeologist leading the Arabs to victory. To the public, tired and exhausted by the horrors of the Western Front, it was a welcome story.

Thomas and Chase had arrived in Palestine in early 1918, looking for a positive story to present to the American public. They arrived in Jerusalem with official British government approval and soon had access to General Allenby and his staff. Allenby and his army had recently captured Jerusalem,

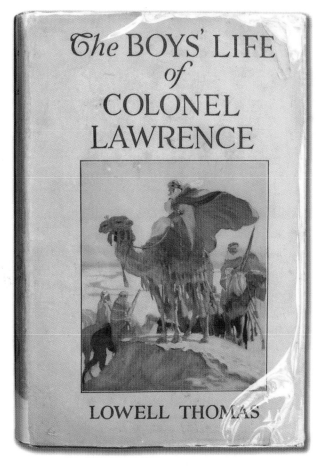

Best selling Lawrence books by Lowell Thomas.
On left, an English edition by Hutchinson,
on right, an American edition by Century.

and the press, much to Allenby's disdain, was calling it a liberation of the Holy City and likening it to a modern Crusade. While in Jerusalem, Ronald Storrs introduced Thomas to Lawrence. He was invited to visit Lawrence at Akaba. By the end of March, Thomas and Chase arrived, taking numerous photographs of the British and Arab troops, and meeting Feisal, Auda and other important tribal leaders. Lawrence made arrangements for the visit to go smoothly and even set up a side expedition to Petra. By April 10th, Thomas and Chase were leaving Akaba for Egypt, after taking over two hundred photographs and interviewing many of the members of the British staff. Judging by the locations of the photographs taken of Lawrence and by his travel diary, Thomas and he likely spent no more than three days together. They did meet again at Arab Bureau headquarters in Cairo some time in late April or early May.

Thomas opened his travelogue show in London, having been convinced to bring it there, instead of playing to American audiences. Seeing the popularity of the Arabian half of the show, he added more images to it, even getting Lawrence to don his Arab robes and pose for additional photographs. Lawrence made several visits to the Thomas flat in Wimbledon and seemed to be quite taken by the publicity. He also realized that a higher public image

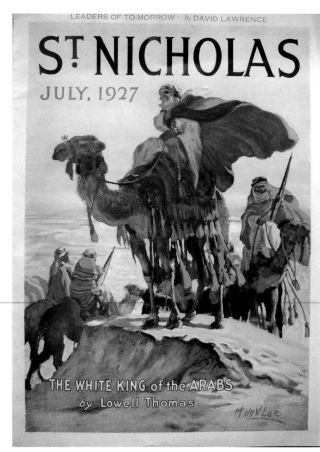

Lawrence stories by Lowell Thomas continued to appear in many magazines including this 1927 cover story of St. Nicholas.

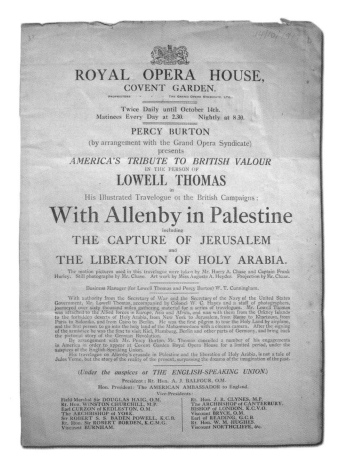

Travelogue program from the Royal Opera House before Lawrence was added to the title, October, 1919.

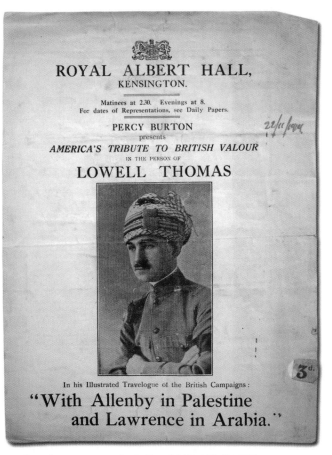

Travelogue program from Royal Albert Hall with Lawrence gaining title billing with Allenby. November, 1919.

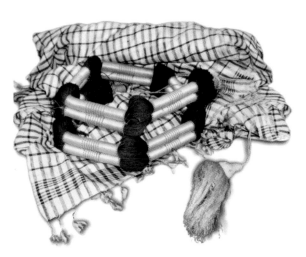

Agal and keffiyeh brought back from Akaba by Lowell Thomas. The keffiyeh appears in several photographs of Thomas and Chase.

Harry Chase, taken in London during the Lawrence photo shoot. Chase was already a well-known photographer and magic lantern projectionist when he went to work for Lowell Thomas.

Harry Chase filming near Akaba, 1918.

would strengthen his own influence on official government policy. During Lawrence's lifetime, Thomas would downplay how much involvement with the travelogue Lawrence had, even stating that Chase had to trick the shy Lawrence into photographing him. During the London run of the show, Allenby, Feisal and his staff, and many of Lawrence's fellow officers and men came to see the travelogue. Lawrence attended one performance with Hubert

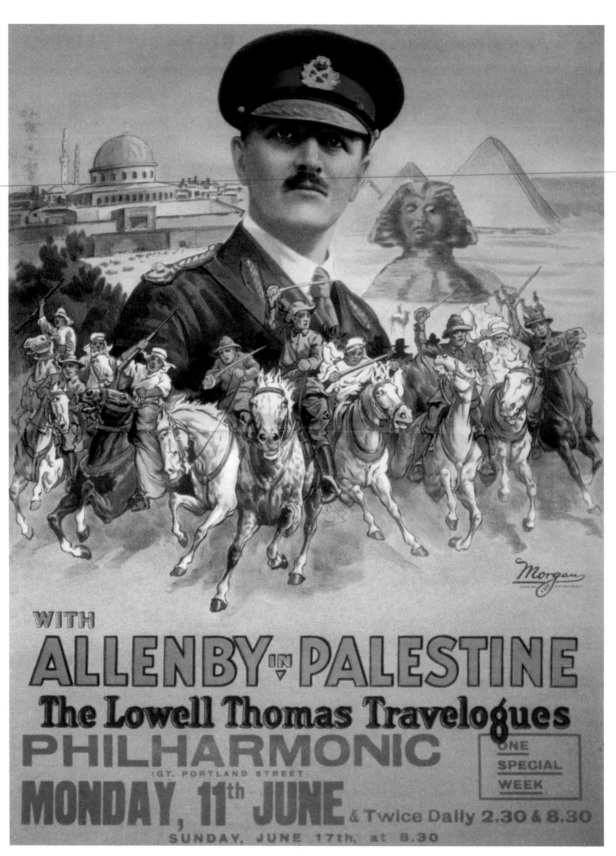

Poster of the Allenby travelogue.

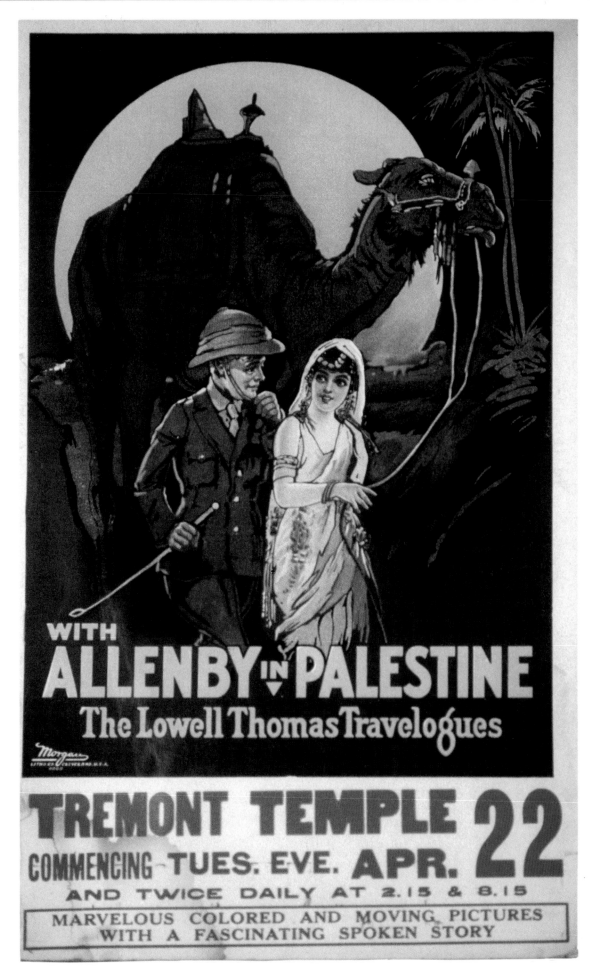

Small poster of the Allenby travelogue.

Young, who served with him in the Hejaz. When Thomas made reference that only Lawrence was up front leading the Arabs, Young objected to it. Lawrence knew that wasn't true. Lawrence promised Young he would speak to Thomas about the omission, but when Young saw the show again, nothing had been changed.

Though Lawrence was now able to take advantage of what the publicity offered, it also brought on intense public and press attention that he soon began to loathe. The Thomas story avoided all of the political double-dealings and broken promises. Lawrence would try to resolve some of this working with Winston Churchill at the upcoming Cairo Conference and try to present a clearer picture of his role in his planned book, *The Seven Pillars of Wisdom*.

For the post-war public though, the legend was born. Thomas followed up his travelogue by writing his own book, the immensely successful *With Lawrence in Arabia*. Filled with exaggeration and hyperbole with a scattering of truth, it supplemented the romantic image that the travelogue had started. It is the photographic record of Harry Chase that remains so strong even today. His still photographs and motion picture film provide us a very strong record of the men and locations of the Arab Revolt. His photographic sessions with Lawrence in London produced the most well known iconic images of *'Lawrence of Arabia.'*

Hand tinted lantern slides used for the travelogue. The slides were tinted by Augusta Heyder, a young woman from New Jersey and recognized as the best slide painter in the country. Nearly 300 slides would be used in the travelogue. Many reviewers raved about being awed and overwhelmed by the colorful images.

Lawrence in the Royal Air Force blue service uniform. Lawrence urged Lord Trenchard, Chief of Staff of the RAF, to eliminate the impractical high collared tunic and the required swagger stick to be carried by other ranks. Eventually these changes were made.

-Lawrence in the Ranks-

For an army officer to join the Royal Air Force as an aircraftman, a private, was unheard of. For Lieutenant-Colonel T. E. Lawrence C.B., D.S.O. to change names and join the service in anonymity was puzzling to even his close friends. George Bernard Shaw called it "*a maddening masquerade.*" Churchill and many of his government colleagues felt Lawrence's enlistment was a waste of his talents. Lawrence did not provide any satisfactory answer to his friends on why he joined the ranks but that he simply wanted to do it. He was comfortable with the ranks. In the Hejaz, he gathered the Camel Corps soldiers around him and spoke plainly of the mission they faced. The enlisted men were not used to the level approach. There wasn't an obvious class divide that many officers had. After the war, Lawrence went out of his way in helping enlisted men who had served with him find employment, writing letters of recommendation, and offering words of encouragement. Perhaps the time in the ranks would keep his day busy while his mind could tackle other interests. This provided an escape from the popular Lawrence of Arabia creation, a degrading to a lower level, a self-inflicted punishment. His mental condition was fragile too, brought on by reliving the nightmare of Deraa and coming to terms with his illegitimacy.

In August 1922 Lawrence joined the Royal Air Force. He had been planning to do so since January. He felt he could write a book about his experience in the ranks. Lawrence had completed the text of the *Seven Pillars* and it was now being seen by friends for comment and revision. His powerful friends in the Royal Air Force handled anticipated difficulties with his enlistment. He could not even pass the physical and special arrangements allowed him in. Enlisting under the assumed name of John Hume Ross, he was sent to Uxbridge for training. Not completely healed from the injuries suffered in a plane crash, Lawrence managed to get through the rigors of 3 months of basic training. He found comfort in being with this group of men and after his training he was sent to an RAF school of photography. At this same time, Lawrence kept busy commissioning more illustrations for the *Seven Pillars of Wisdom*. This balancing between the duties of an aircraftman in training with the needs to finish his book perhaps led to his identity being discovered. By mid-December, reporters were at the RAF station looking for Lawrence. Two weeks later headlines told of Lawrence of Arabia, the war hero enlisting as a private. Determining the situation was impossible to continue, the Secretary of State for Air, Sir Samuel Hoare, ordered Lawrence discharged.

Trenchard offered Lawrence a commission in the RAF suggesting he work with armoured cars. Lawrence remained adamant about wanting to return to the ranks. With the help of Sir Philip Chetwode, a general of the Palestine campaign, Lawrence joined the Tank Corps as Private T. E. Shaw. He was stationed at Bovington, in Dorset. At this time, Lawrence became deeply depressed, a condition pushed further by being kicked out of the RAF and finding his situation in the Tanks Corps close to intolerable. Lawrence arranged for a young man to beat and whip him, delivering a punishment he felt he deserved, an occasional arrangement he would make for the rest of his life. His brother Arnold commented later that in some way it was Lawrence's way of being punished like the medieval saints he admired. They flogged their bodies to keep them in subjection. Today, with a growing understanding of post-traumatic stress, we can be sympathetic to his behavior. He also hinted at thoughts of suicide to some friends. Lawrence would get some relief by taking long and intense rides on his motorcycle, reaching high speeds. He also found refuge at his newly rented cottage of Clouds Hill, a small place in desperate need of repair. It offered a retreat, soon filled with favorite books and records. There he would entertain a few close army friends and use the space to assemble his *Seven Pillars of Wisdom*. But he still wanted out of the Tank Corps. Finally, with the urging of many friends including Churchill, George Bernard Shaw and John Buchan appealing to the Prime Minister Stanley Baldwin himself, a transfer was arranged back to the Royal Air Force.

Getting back into the RAF had an immediate effect on Lawrence. He was assigned to the Cadet College at Cranwell where he would serve from August 1925 until November 1926. His duties required him to help take care of the aero-

Physical Examination for Lawrence's entry into the Royal Air Force. Lawrence was not physically fit and special arrangements were made for him to pass the physical. He lied about his age. He's listed at 28 years old instead of 34. Some scars are noted and his height is listed as 5 foot 5 1/2inches.

planes the cadets would fly. His mental health improved as he began to work leisurely, even happily in his new duties and in the relationships with his officers and men. He found time to finish off the lavish subscribers edition of *Seven Pillars of Wisdom* and prepared the deeply edited abridged edition *Revolt in the Desert* for publication. Knowing the intense publicity the books would bring him, Lawrence applied for a posting overseas. He was transferred to India in December.

Lawrence was stationed at the RAF Depot at Karachi, working on aeroplane engine overhauls. With his writing skills, he quickly assumed the duties of clerk typist. He was in the middle of almost nowhere, surrounded by desert. He was kept informed of the great reception of his books. The tremendous sales of *Revolt in the Desert* quickly paid off his large debt built up in producing the *Seven Pillars of Wisdom*. He arranged for any additional profit to go to an RAF charity. While in India, he had time to work on his notes for his autobiographical book *The Mint*, based on his earlier experiences in the RAF. Lawrence looked on this book as a tribute

to the RAF but Air Marshall Trenchard preferred Lawrence delay in publishing it. Not wanting to put his RAF career again in jeopardy, he agreed to wait. It would be published in 1955. By May 1928 Lawrence asked to be transferred to the remote base at Miranshah, near the border of Afghanistan. This was essentially a fortress surrounded by barbed wire, protecting the border manned by 31 RAF personal and 700 Indian Scouts. Lawrence commented, "*I like this place. It feels as though I'd dropped over the world's rim out of sight.*" The obscure location gave Lawrence enough spare time away from his clerk duties to work on translating Homer's *Odyssey*, a job proposed to him by the American book collector Ralph Isham. Bruce Rogers would print his highly praised translation in 1932.

When Afghanistan erupted in revolt in 1928, a press story reported that Lawrence of Arabia and the Government of India were behind it. The story stated Lawrence

Aircraftman Shaw

'AIRCRAFTMAN SHAW'
in 'Scruff order'
Copyright

Karachi Feb. 1927.

Lawrence at Karachi.
This photograph was annotated by Lawrence.

developed between Lawrence and the Smith family. Lawrence became a welcomed member of the family, enjoying picnics and social outings. Sydney's wife Clare, felt an especially close friendship with Lawrence, enjoying rides in the small speedboat the *Biscuit* and his love of classical music. Even the family dogs liked his company. The next three years would be happy ones for Lawrence, recounted by Clare Sydney Smith in her memoir *The Golden Reign*.

Lawrence acted as a personal clerk to Sydney Smith. He was of great assistance in the Schneider Cup races, taking well to the sea and working with boats and seaplanes. He did anger some politicians and Air Force officials who were bothered by his casual interactions with important racing figures and celebrities. He needed to take a less visible role or risk being thrown out of the Royal Air Force again.

was a disguised spy in Afghanistan, working the borders and studying its tribes. The Foreign Office denied the absurd allegations. Unaware of the controversy, Lawrence was putting in 14-hour days, splitting the time between RAF duties and translating Homer. There was growing pressure to have Lawrence removed from the area. On January 12, 1929, with no publicity on his destination, Lawrence sailed for England.

When his ship arrived in England effort was made to avoid the press but they succeeded in filming him coming down the ladder. Within weeks an angered Lawrence went to Parliament to confront the politicians who made the accusations of him spying in Afghanistan. Accepting his explanations, the meeting ended on good terms. In March, Lawrence was posted to the RAF Flying Boat Station at Cattewater. The commanding officer, a friend, was Wing-Commander Sydney Smith. A special friendship

Lawrence in the Tank Corps outside Hut 12, May or June 1923.
Photo by B. Butler.

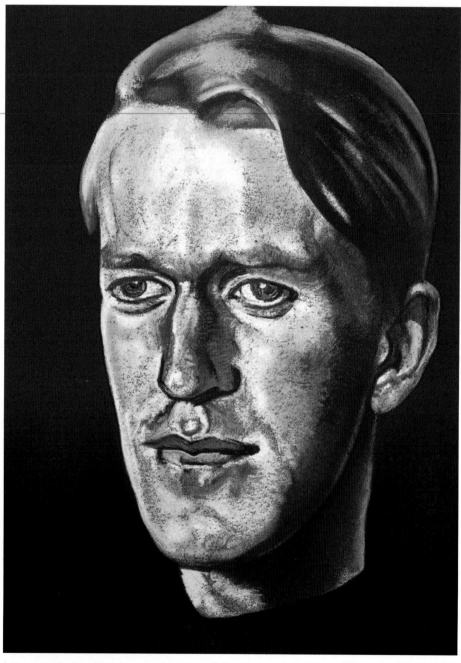

Lawrence by Eric Kennington. This is one of the many commission pastel portraits Kennington produced for Lawrence's book.

-Seven Pillars of Wisdom-

From an early age Lawrence had ambitions to be a writer. During his days at Carchemish he prepared a book about seven cities of the Middle East to be titled *Seven Pillars of Wisdom*. The title is based on a verse from the Book of Proverbs 9:1: *"Wisdom hath builded her house; she hath hewn out her seven pillars."* Unsatisfied with this book, he claims to have destroyed it. The Arab Revolt gave him the needed subject for his book. Lawrence would use this title for his account of the history of the Arab Revolt and his own role in it. Lawrence set his standards high. He didn't want to write a war memoir. He wanted to write a literary masterpiece.

Lawrence started writing his book while in Paris in January 1919 during the Peace Conference. He briefly left Paris in May to fly to Cairo to consult the Arab Bureau papers to help with details needed for his book. On this trip, the Handley Page bomber he was travelling in crashed outside of Rome killing two and wounding him. Eventually he made it to Egypt. Lawrence com-

pleted his first draft of 200,000 words by the end of July. Returning to England, he started to circulate his manuscript for criticism and historical assessment.

He was returning with his manuscript from visiting Alan Dawnay, a wartime colleague and friend. While changing trains at Reading Station, Lawrence left his official briefcase containing the manuscript, his war photographs and negatives in the coffee shop. It was never found. Lawrence was devastated. With the urging of friends, particularly Hogarth, he started over. In the attic of 14 Barton Street, near Westminster Abbey, working long hours, often without sleep and food, he wrote it again. This version he would revise over the next two years, essentially making a third text.

Lawrence started negotiating selling an abridged version of his book to the American publisher F. N. Doubleday but changed his mind. He went back to the thought of putting out a lavish, limited edition, specially printed book. He had a longtime interest in fine book printing and getting *Seven Pillars* produced would

Lawrence instructing a Stokes mortar class. Akaba, 1917. The English soldier is Corporal Brook. HMS Humber can be seen in the background. Photograph supplied to Cosmo Clark.

occupy much of his spare time over the next five years.

Lawrence wanted the book to be illustrated by the leading young artists of England. He had seen the paintings of Eric Kennington, a veteran of the Western Front, and approached him about doing some work for him. Kennington had seen the Lowell Thomas production and was enthusiastic about the task but wanted to go the Middle East and work from life, not photographs. Shortly, Lawrence arranged for his visit and Kennington was soon doing pastel portraits of Auda and other colorful Arab personalities. Lawrence was greatly impressed by his work and Kennington became art editor to Lawrence's planned limited edition of *Seven Pillars*. Lawrence commissioned work from the leading English artists of the time. Contemporary artists Paul Nash, William Roberts, Colin Gill and Henry Lamb joined established artists Augustus John, William Nicolson, William Rothenstein and John Singer Sargent in making contributions to Lawrence's book.

Lawrence was still struggling with the text. He kept sending it to trusted friends for advice and revision suggestions. His friends continually reassured him how great it was while Lawrence routinely told them how rotten he thought it was. Lawrence had eight copies printed up of his revised version. He did not want to risk losing it again. Referred to as the Oxford Text, it would be this version that would be finally edited to the final printed subscribers edition.

In December 1922, now in the RAF, Lawrence once again considered selling an abridged version of his book, this time to the English publisher Jonathan Cape. Lawrence felt

Cosmo Clark's drawing titled Stokes Gun Class at Akaba.

he could get enough money to leave the RAF, start up his own dream of a private press and end his literary frustration with his book. George Bernard Shaw wanted Lawrence to publish the entire book, unabridged, in a strictly limited edition. Cape was furious with Lawrence when he changed his mind again, cancelling plans for an abridgement. Lawrence was soon out of the RAF and joined the Tank Corps, while still making arrangements for more portraits and soliciting comments from friends about his book.

In December 1923, Lawrence met with trusted friends Alan Dannay, D. G. Hogarth and Lionel Curtis laying out publishing plans and financial needs to get the *Seven Pillars*

Lawrence supplied the artists working on illustrations for his Seven Pillars of Wisdom *with many photographs from the Arab campaign. He provided William Roberts with a number of his own photographs of Feisal's army, inspiring the painting* Camel March.

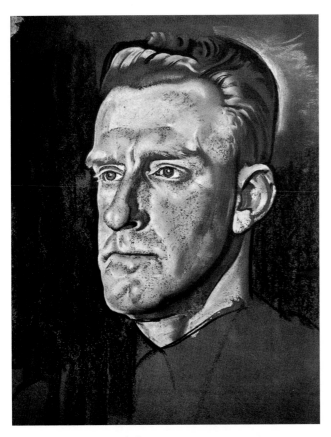

Boyle by Eric Kennington
Boyle was Senior Naval Officer, Red Sea.

Jaafar Pasha by Eric Kennington.
Jaafar was C.-in-C. of the Arab Northern Army.

out. It was decided to publish one hundred copies at 30 pounds each. A number of incomplete copies would also be made for gifts for men who had served with Lawrence during the war and could not afford such an expensive book.

Printers and bookbinders were found who could work to the high standard demanded by Lawrence. The printing was closely supervised by Lawrence. He would revise some text so that each page finished with a complete line of text and the end of a paragraph. The cost of the project was running way over budget and more subscriptions were offered. To save the production, Lawrence went back to Cape and offered another abridged version, this time it would not be published until after Lawrence released his completed limited edition. This arrangement

Camel March by William Roberts.

gave the financial security to finish the job. Cape also agreed to stop selling the abridgement once Lawrence had made enough money to pay off his debt. Lawrence was now commissioning more art for tailpieces and illustrations to use in the text.

Almost every copy was different. The leading binders of England were used to complete production. Lawrence signed every copy T. E. Shaw. The initial copies were finished in December 1926. King George V was presented the first copy. Lawrence gave gifts to some friends, presented "incomplete" copies to some veterans of the Hejaz campaign. In all, a total of 211 copies were printed at a cost of over 13000 pounds. In March 1927, Cape issued the abridgement *Revolt in the Desert*. It sold over 90,000 copies in four months. Lawrence refused any profit once his debt was paid off and directed his trustees to give the additional profit to the RAF Benevolent Fund. He then asked Cape to stop publishing the book during his lifetime.

Immediately after Lawrence's death, his brother Arnold allowed the *Seven Pillars of Wisdom* to be published for the general public. By September 1935, 100,000 copies were in print. It has remained in print since then. Winston Churchill said, "*It ranks with the greatest books written in the English language.*"

Matar by Eric Kennington.

Emir Abdulla by Eric Kennington.

Auda abu Tayi by Eric Kennington.

Emir Shakir by Eric Kennington.

Abdulla el Zaagi by Eric Kennington.

An Ageyli (Hamud) by Eric Kennington.

Serj el Ateibi by Eric Kennington.

Lawrence at the Smith's rented seaside cottage at Thurlestone, Devon. 1931.

-Last years in the Royal Air Force-

After the Schneider Cup, Lawrence turned his attention to air-sea rescue boats. His interest in developing fast boats may have been sparked by his work on his speedboat. By the fall of 1930 Lawrence was closely working with Flight-Lieutenant Beauforte-Greenwood, Head of the Air Ministry's Marine Equipment branch. Lawrence and the Smiths witnessed a fatal air crash in the waters of Plymouth Sound. In perfect weather conditions, an Iris III flying boat taking firing practice nose-dived into the sea. Lawrence and Smith did their best getting to the crash site, using a slow launch. Lawrence immediately took over the rescue attempt, diving into the water, helping to save six of the twelve airmen on board. Later at the inquest into the accident, Lawrence gave his low opinion of the flying officer in charge of the aircraft. The rescue attempt pointed out the need for faster air-speed rescue boats to help in situations just like this.

This accident focused Lawrence's attention even more on the development of stronger engines and faster boats. He was teamed with Hubert Scott-Paine of the British Power Boat Company. It was now Lawrence the mechanic that took over. He had incredible curiosity and insight into mechanical workings. The same fascination he had with improving his motorcycle's performance is found with his mastering of boat engines and design. The task left him with little spare time. He writes:

> Picture me just as a sailor, now-a-days, working so hard all the bright hours that in the evening I just bath and bed. No Homer; and no letters.

Lawrence helped develop the prototype design of the new tender and put it and its engines through long hours of testing. This boat would become the RAF 200 Class

Aircraftman Shaw with Clare Sydney Smith in his powerboat Biscuit.

Seaplane Tender, a prototype of the P T boats used during World War II. His writing skills would lead him to put together the technically clear instruction manual for the Seaplane Tender. Lawrence's skills were also needed in designing floating targets. These would be towed behind launches for aircraft to take target practice on. He tackled these projects with an always-growing aptitude to the task. Though his rank was just an aircraftman, it was only low in title. His responsibility and assignment was much greater, consulting with high-ranking officers and designers to whom he put forth his welcomed suggestions.

He had a much greater freedom now. Though limited on how much spare time he had, Lawrence made great use of it. He was able to take his Brough Superior out on visits to his well-known friends, the Shaws, Lady Astor and others. He did his best to keep up his correspondence and his letters from this period show what satisfaction the mechanical phase of his life had given him. In a 1931 letter to T. C. Griffin, a veteran of the Hejaz campaign, he recalled the long ago war:

I am so old now, and it feels a lifetime away. Nine years ago I enlisted, and have not thought about the Middle East since. The Air Force life suits me, and I'm happy in it.

Lawrence faced a forced retirement from the Royal Air Force in March 1935. He disclosed mixed feelings about his leaving to his friends. To Liddell Hart, who had just published a biography of Lawrence, he was very positive about his leaving. Lawrence said he was looking forward to true

Lawrence with one of the Smith's family dogs.

Page from a photographic scrapbook presented to Lawrence by the British Powerboat Company documenting his work with the development of high-speed air sea rescue launches.

Aircraftman Shaw and his commanding officer and friend Wing Commander Sydney Smith.

leisure and hoped it would be like *"a great Sunday that goes on and on."* To other friends he shared his fear of loneliness. In a revealing passage to his friend Ronald Storrs he wrote,

After my discharge I have somehow to pick up a new life and occupy myself–but beforehand it looks and feels like an utterly blank wall. Old age coming, I suppose; at any rate I can admit to being quite a bit afraid for myself, which is quite a new feeling. Up till now I've never come to the end of anything.

Title page from the Bruce Rogers designed Odyssey, translated by Lawrence while in the RAF. The highly acclaimed, well-designed book used scented ink in the printing of the gold roundels and some copies even today have a scent.

Before his departure, Lawrence looked back at his RAF duties and felt pleased with his many accomplishments. He wrote what was essentially a thank you note to John Buchan to forward to Stanley Baldwin, the former Prime Minister who arranged for Lawrence to enter the RAF. Lawrence said that his RAF years provided him with the only really contented years of his life. He had done his best to raise the pride and respect of the ranks. He writes of his own jobs of aeroplane engine work in India, his involvement with the 1929 Schneider Cup race, and the four or five years work with developing marine-craft boats for the RAF. He thanks them for gratifying his indulgence, how satisfying the twelve years of service has been, and how he feels hopelessly in their debt.

On February 26, 1935 Lawrence left Bridlington on his bicycle, and headed towards Clouds Hill into retirement. He was forty-six.

Brough Superior ad featuring Lawrence.

-Lawrence and his Motorcycles-

Of the many interests that Lawrence had, perhaps he was most enthusiastic about his motorcycles. They combined his curiosity for things mechanical and his passion for speed.

His mother made a note of having sent his first motorcycle to him while he was in Cairo. She felt he was going to take it to Carchemish. During the war, Ernest Dowson, the Director-General of the Survey of Egypt, recalls Lawrence travelling on his motorcycle at Giza and Bulaq. Additional confirmation of his motorcycling in Egypt comes from a letter to Lawrence, in the Bodleian collection, from Norman Dewhurst noting that it was he who was loaned Lawrence's two stroke Triumph and that he also made some repairs to it while in Cairo.

In late November of 1922, Lawrence informed the artist William Roberts that he bought secondhand *an old crock of a Triumph.*" By the end of the year he had given that bike to a service friend and purchased his first Brough Superior, a Mark I model. He would own seven Brough Superiors with an eighth on order at the time of his death. Lawrence named

Roy Reiffer on George III, T. E.'s *Brough Superior RK 899.*
Mr. Reiffer owned the Red Garage in Bovington, near Clouds Hill, where T. E. bought his gas.

Lawrence on George V, RK4907, 1925-26.

them George I, and II and so on after George Brough, the owner of the company that made them. The first machine brought him much pleasure. He noted, *"it goes 80 mph and is a perfect thing."* He was able to use this machine for his trips from camp and into London. Forced to leave the RAF and short of funds, Lawrence felt he would have to sell his motorcycle but avoided giving it up. He had the machine when he was allowed to enlist in the Tank Corps and described how much it meant to him in a letter to Edward Garnett,

My motor-bike is called into use when I find myself on parade facing an unconscious sergeant with my fists hard clenched. A hundred fast miles seem to make camp feel less confined afterwards.

At the end of March 1923, Lawrence crashed this bike describing the accident to Hogarth,

Ran over a broken glass bottle at speed, burst front tyre, ran up a bank & turned over. Damage to self nil; to bike somewhat. There goes my power of breaking bounds.

Lawrence bought George II some time in 1923. This bike had a sidecar he could attach and he would make some journeys with his Tank Corps friends. Some of his colleagues were impressed by the machine and its cost, but all noted his skill and fearlessness as a rider. In the Bovington camp he became known as 'Broughie' Shaw. By the end of the year this machine was borrowed and wrecked beyond repair.

By February 1924, Lawrence was driving the new model SS80 bought from the Brough dealer in Croydon. This bike would provide him with numerous rides around the countryside with him keeping detailed logs of the time travelled. In March 1925 Lawrence was ready to move on to a stronger bike being introduced by Brough, the SS. 100. On April 4th, he paid just under two hundred pounds for his new bike, George IV, and some accessories. This was his bike while he shifted out of the Tank Corps and back to the RAF in July 1925. Lawrence writes to John Buchan of this bike going 108 miles an hour. He only kept it for a short time, however and by October, he was trading it in for George V, a 1926 model SS. 100.

There are many photographs of Lawrence riding George V. This is the machine, RK 4907, he used to take many

*Returning from India, Lawrence obtained George VI, UL656,
pictured with George Brough, 1930.*

rides from Cranwell to London. It's also the machine he is riding when he races the Bristol Fighter, described in *The Mint*. He went on a seven and a half hour journey to Edinburgh to check on the maps being made for *Seven Pillars of Wisdom*. In September Lawrence wrote George Brough a thank you letter for providing four years of solid pleasure.

He also provided a letter of endorsement for Brough to use in any advertisement he chose fit, with the condition that he wait until mid-December when Lawrence would be on his way to India. Before he left, Lawrence crashed this Brough, banging up his kneecap and recouped a hundred pounds for it.

Lawrence absolutely enjoyed riding. His words would bring joy to any motorcyclist. As he wrote to Robert Graves in 1927:

The greatest pleasure of my recent life has been speed on the road.
The bike would do 100 m.p.h. but I'm not a racing man. It was my satisfaction to purr along between 60 and 70 m.p.h. and drink in the air and the general view. I lose detail at even moderate speeds but gain comprehension. When I used to cross Salisbury Plain at 50 or so, I'd feel the earth moulding herself under me. It was me piling up this hill, hollowing this valley, stretching out this level place: almost the earth came alive, heaving and tossing on each side like a sea. That's a thing the slow coach will never feel. It is the reward of Speed. I could write for hours on the lustfulness of moving swiftly.

Lawrence returned from India in late January 1929. Charlotte Shaw and some friends had hoped to buy Lawrence a Brough for his return to England but Lawrence insisted on paying for the new bike himself. The new SS 100, UL 656, was delivered the first week of February. Lawrence was soon stationed at Cattewater and making many trips to London and back on George VI. Before the end of June he had logged 4000 miles on it.

By March 1932, Lawrence arranged with George Brough to trade in this bike George VI, for his last bike, a 1932 model SS 100, GW 2275, with many modifications made for him. George VII would provide Lawrence with many hours of riding. He would tend to minor repairs himself, make suggestions for improvements to Brough, and stop by the shop in Nottingham for major repair work. By July 1934, he had 25000 miles on it. At the time of his fatal crash on this bike, his new Brough Superior, George VIII, was ready for delivery.

Lawrence and George Brough.

Lawrence on George VII, GW2275, the motorcycle he was riding when he had his fatal crash.

Postcard of Clouds Hill printed shortly after the property was given to the National Trust.

The Clouds Hill book room.
Lawrence installed the fireplace in September 1933.
He designed the reading chair, the stainless steel book rest
and fireplace fender. This photograph was part of a series
taken of Clouds Hill by Walton Adams,
shortly after Lawrence's death.

The upstairs music room. Lawrence's large gramophone can
be seen on the left. The painting by Gilbert Spencer, made for
Lawrence, is mounted in the wood paneling above the window.
At his desk are a despatch case and a small silver model of a
RAF seaplane. Behind the desk are his typewriter and a small
painted model of the powerboat the Biscuit.

-Clouds Hill-

It's a cottage, a half-ruined cottage, near camp, where I have a room for writing in. A pretty little place, & quiet: among trees, & opening on the heath.

Letter home, 19.xii.23

In 1923, while in the Tank Corps stationed at Bovington, Lawrence found a small cottage to rent. Located a mile from camp, and in need of repair, it would be a perfect place for him to work on his *Seven Pillars of Wisdom*. Clouds Hill was built in 1808 as a workman's cottage. It had remained unoccupied for a number of years before Lawrence rented it. About twenty feet by ten feet, this secluded structure was nestled in trees, off a small road, yet easily within walking distance of camp.

Lawrence had to make immediate repairs to make it livable once again. He focused first on repairing the roof and getting the top floor ready to serve as a writing room. In time, this cottage would house his major collection of books and records. He soon had friends visiting, including George Bernard Shaw and his wife Charlotte, E. M. Foster and Thomas Hardy. Clouds Hill also provided a welcome place to visit by some of his friends from the ranks. It was very basic, with no running water or indoor toilet. With no kitchen, when any food was served, it was mostly out of tins. Drinks, with no alcohol allowed, consisted of a blend of China tea or water.

Eventually Lawrence had the downstairs room finished off to be his book room and sleeping area. The walls were lined with bookcases and a custom built reading chair was placed near the fireplace.

Upstairs became the music room, housing an expensive and large gramophone and his record collection including recordings of his favorites, Bach, Mozart, Beethoven and Elgar. A leather covered sofa, armchairs and writing table were placed there.

When Lawrence got closer to retirement from the Royal Air Force, more funds were put into remodeling Clouds Hill. Lawrence designed a ram device designed for bringing fresh water to the cottage. He also had a glass covered enclosed pool built to serve as a small swimming pool, but more importantly to be a ready source of water to put out any grass fires that were common during the dry summers. He put in a toilet and bathtub with the latest hot water tank. He enjoyed long hot baths. To provide more daylight to the small back room, he installed a large porthole salvaged from HMS *Tiger*.

Part of his large collection of books included many volumes inscribed to him by his author friends. The cottage also housed his small collection of fine art, with paintings by Henry Tuke and Gilbert Spencer. He also obtained portraits of his two wartime leaders; the Eric Kennington portrait of General Allenby and the Augustus John portrait of Emir Feisal. Over the years, Lawrence had custom-crafted decorative arts made, including candlesticks, a fireplace fender and book rest. Among the small special objects he kept at the cottage were a silver model of a seaplane, another of the Schneider Cup racing plane, and a beautifully detailed model of his speedboat, the *Biscuit*.

His brother Arnold left Clouds Hill to the National Trust in 1938.

Doorway and lintel. The lintel, carved by Lawrence, with the Greek works translated to mean, "Why worry?"

LT.-COL. T. E. LAWRENCE, C.B., D.S.O., M.C.

Lawrence by James McBey. 1918.
Book Plate from Nile to Aleppo by Hector W. Dinning, published in 1920.
The Lawrence title includes M.C. however Lawrence
was not awarded the Military Cross.

-Portraits of Lawrence-

James McBey was already an acclaimed artist when he was attached to Allenby's army as an official war artist. The art world had looked on the Scottish printmaker as a successor to James McNeil Whistler. While with the Egyptian Expeditionary Force, he had gone out on patrol with the Camel Corps, documented the surrender of Jerusalem, and sketched many portraits of soldiers and generals. He accompanied the British Army into Damascus. McBey most likely painted Lawrence soon after his meeting with Feisal and Allenby. Lawrence would leave Damascus the next day. McBey recounts that when Lawrence was sitting for this portrait, Arabs would come in and kiss his hand, bidding him

T. E. *Lawrence by Augustus John.* 1919

farewell. Lawrence, in his Arab robes, is shown gaunt and physically strained. By the capture of Damascus, Lawrence said he was *"emotionally and physically spent."* There is remarkable similarity to this portrait and the photograph by John Findlay, taken on the balcony of the Victoria Hotel, most likely on the same day.

Writing about Lawrence in Damascus, Liddell Hart states, "His *dark mood in these days of triumph made an indelible impression on his companions and, because of their affection, grieved them."* Responding to this sentence, Lawrence writes on the typescript to Hart,

Did you ever see McBey's portrait of me (in the Imperial War Museum) painted in Damascus a day after we got in? It is shockingly strange to me.

Though Lawrence would sit for other artists wearing his Arab robes, this McBey portrait is the only one painted from life during wartime, painted as he appeared, not dressing up for the part.

Augustus John, in 1919, was recognized as one of the best of the British portrait artists. He was sent to Paris to cover the Peace Conference. An Honorary Major attached to the Canadian Army, John was lent a friend's apartment to use as a studio at 60 Avenue Montaigne. This studio would be visited by a large number of dignitaries

Lawrence arrived in Paris by mid January. In March, Feisal and Lawrence visited John at the studio and had portraits painted there. Lawrence came back for more sittings, with John producing three known oil portraits and seven sketches. John thought Lawrence *"enjoyed being painted and always seemed tickled by the result."*

T. E. *Lawrence by William Orpen.* 1919.

T. E. *Lawrence by William Rothenstein*. 1920-22.

These Peace Conference portraits show Lawrence wearing the full set of Arab robes and dagger. While officially as part of Feisal's staff, in Paris, Lawrence would wear his British officer's uniform and the Arab headdress. He donned the robes in John's studio though and from those sittings we owe the best-known paintings of Lawrence.

John and Lawrence stayed on friendly terms, socially and artistically. When Feisal came to London, John tried to arrange a visit with Lawrence and him. One of John's portraits of Feisal was purchased by Lawrence and served as a frontispiece in *Seven Pillars of Wisdom*. John continued to do more paintings and drawings of Lawrence through his Royal Air Force career as well. John was even looking forward to working more with Lawrence after his retirement from the RAF.

During the Peace Conference, Lawrence also spent time sitting for William Orpen, another well-known society portrait painter. His studio was at the Hotel Astoria where Orpen painted or sketched over forty-six important visitors. Lawrence went for two sessions of ninety minutes each. Lawrence is painted wearing a suit coat and tie. It was an interesting choice for the portrait because Lawrence, most of the time in Paris, would have worn his uniform. It could be that Orpen choose not to romanticize that Lawrence, avoiding the robes and even the uniform. Instead, Orpen painted Lawrence the diplomat. Lawrence didn't think highly of this painting but his mother did. After Lawrence died, she even tried to buy it, but it was already in a private collection.

Lawrence by William Roberts. 1922.
Roberts produced several highly acclaimed line drawings and portraits for Seven Pillars of Wisdom.
This portrait was completed in December 1922 during Lawrence's first stay in the RAF.

Derwent Wood was also sent to Paris to record his artistic impressions. Wood was a sculptor and he had been requested to do busts of Wilson, Clemenceau and Foch. He also sought out Lawrence. The Lawrence bust was displayed as part of the Royal Academy Summer Show of 1920 where Lawrence did get to view it. He did not heavily endorse it.

William Rothenstein completed the only full-length portrait painting of Lawrence wearing Arab robes. This painting was started in the summer of 1920 with Lawrence still doing more sittings for it into the spring of 1922. When finally completed, Lawrence brought his mother and brother Arnold to Rothenstein's studio to view the painting. Lawrence told the artist that this was his mother's preferred painting of all the portraits.

Of all the British artists, it is Eric Kennington that is so intertwined with Lawrence. In the fall of 1920, a London gallery showed Kennington's war work. Lawrence was very taken with it and bought two pieces. Kennington was flattered by the new patron and soon travelled to Oxford to meet Lawrence. In little time, Lawrence was convinced this was the artist he needed to do many of the portraits for *Seven Pillars*. Kennington turned down Lawrence's offer to do portraits working from his large collection of wartime photos. Instead, Kennington wanted to head to Egypt and Arabia to draw the subjects from life. Lawrence was thrilled with the artist's willingness to do this. The resulting work in pastels captured the many Arab subjects in all their finery. On return, Kennington became the Art Editor for *Seven Pillars* and worked with Lawrence in arranging sittings, getting artists, dealing with printers and finalizing proofs.

Kennington's real contribution was his portrayal of Lawrence. Kennington was taken by the romantic story of Lawrence. He had attended the Lowell Thomas travelogue and admits to being captivated by the aura of the "Uncrowned King of Arabia." But Kennington saw in Lawrence much more than that. To Kennington, Lawrence was a true hero, to be admired for his limitless compassion for all living souls. Kennington's first pastel portrait was likely completed in November 1920. In the next few years, Kennington produced some fine caricatures of Lawrence, poking fun at him, for his book. Lawrence liked how they would provide a balance to the seriousness of his writing. In 1926, with Lawrence finishing up the production of *Seven Pillars of Wisdom*, Kennington sculpted a magnificent bust of Lawrence. Lawrence gave him five sittings of thirty minutes each. When Lawrence saw photographs of the completed bust six weeks later, he told Kennington,

It represents not me, but my top moments, those few seconds in which I succeed in thinking myself right out of things.

Kennington would serve as a pallbearer at Lawrence's funeral, representing the art side of his life. Kennington was approached by Lawrence's brother to do a memorial sculpture of Lawrence. He soon started on an effigy, patterned after the medieval tomb sculptures. The finished carved stone sculpture is at St. Martin's Church in Wareham.

Lawrence was fascinated by the creative process and enjoyed the company of artists and writers. By being a willing subject of fine artists, he was an active participant in the creation of the works themselves. He took seriously what the artist would see in him and how he was portrayed in their work. It provided another view to him on how others saw him and it aided with his own constant self-evaluation. He also had some control on the artist's vision. After the war, it was Lawrence who would put on the Arab robes, to pose for the artist. He had no reason to wear the robes anymore, except to see how the artist might view him wearing them. After Lawrence joined the Royal Air Force, almost all portrayals of him are in the common aircraftman's uniform. Very few civilian representations are done. Lawrence sees himself just as an airman. He insists that Lawrence of Arabia had died years ago. However, after Lawrence's death, Kennington chooses this Arab Lawrence to portray, once again in sculpture, capturing the Medieval "Arab Knight," resting in recumbent effigy, with his head on a camel saddle, his hand on his dagger, with his favorite books by his side.

Lawrence bust by Eric Kennington at Jesus College, Oxford.

*Lawrence effigy by Eric Kennington. 1935-39.
St. Martin's Church, Wareham, Dorset.*

452491..WATCN YOUR CREDIT..INTERNATIONAL NEWS PHOTO
SLUG(LAWRENCE)

UNSCATHED IN ARABIAN ADVENTURES,LAWRENCE OF ARABIA,
INJURED ON MOTORCYCLE.

WOOL,ENGLAND.....COLONEL THOMAS E. LAWRENCE,
THE FAMOUS ADVENTURER KNOWN AS "LAWRENE OF ARABIA"
WHO IS NOW AN OFFICER IN THE BRITISH ARMY UNDER
HIS ADOPTED NAME OF T.E. SHAW, AND WHO WAS INJURED
YESTERDAY, MAY 13TH, WHEN HIS MOTORCYCLE COLLIDED
WITH A BICYCLE RIDDEN BY A CHILD. ALTHOUGH NOT
SERIOUSLY INJURED THE IRONY IN THE STORY LIES IN
THE FACT THA LAWRENCE, OR SHAW, ESCAPED UNSCATHED
IN A SERIES OF WILD ADVENTURES IN THE ARABIAN
DESERT AND WAS RIDINGSO PROSAIC A VEHICLE AS A MOTOR-
CYCLE,—WHEN INJURED.
R-5-14-35-10/39

Press photo and news release announcing Lawrence's motorcycle accident.
The release wrongly identifies Lawrence as an officer in the British Army
and states he was not injured seriously.

-Death and Memorial-

Lawrence planned to take his time getting back to Clouds Hill. He would stay at small villages along the way, visiting old friends. In Cambridge he saw his brother Arnold who reported later that his brother seemed relaxed and content, and spoke of plans of book printing. The press had been alerted to Lawrence's end of RAF service and started to stalk out Clouds Hill waiting for his arrival. He was disgusted by the hounding of the press and sought out help from his influential friends to get rid of them. He arrived home in mid-March. Some pressmen again appeared and there was a violent confrontation with a reporter getting a black eye. Lawrence appealed to the head of the Newspapers Proprietors Association to call off their men and leave him in quietude. The reporters were called off.

With his time in the ranks over, Churchill and Lady Astor had hoped that Lawrence would be ready to take on an active role serving the government. There was talk of him reorganizing the Home Defence Forces. His friend Lord Rodd offered him the Secretaryship of the Bank of England. Lawrence declined the offers. In May, he wrote his artist friend Eric Kennington,

> *Days seem to dawn, suns to shine, evenings to follow, and then I sleep. What have I done, what am I going to do, puzzle me and bewilder me. Have you ever been a leaf and fallen from your tree in autumn and been really puzzled about it? That's the feeling.*

He busied getting Clouds Hill in better shape and got his Brough Superior out of storage and tuned up. He worried about having enough money to live on and started a budget allowing certain amounts for food, gas and postage. Only if needed to, would he take on paying jobs like translating or writing.

On the morning of May 13, 1935, Lawrence had to go to the post office in Bovington to mail a package and

Pallbearers escorting Lawrence's coffin. On right side, front to back: Pat Knowles, Colonel Newcombe and Sgt. Bradbury RAF. On the left side: Eric Kennington, Arthur Russell of the Tank Corps and Sir Ronald Storrs. Arnold and Barbara Lawrence follow the coffin.

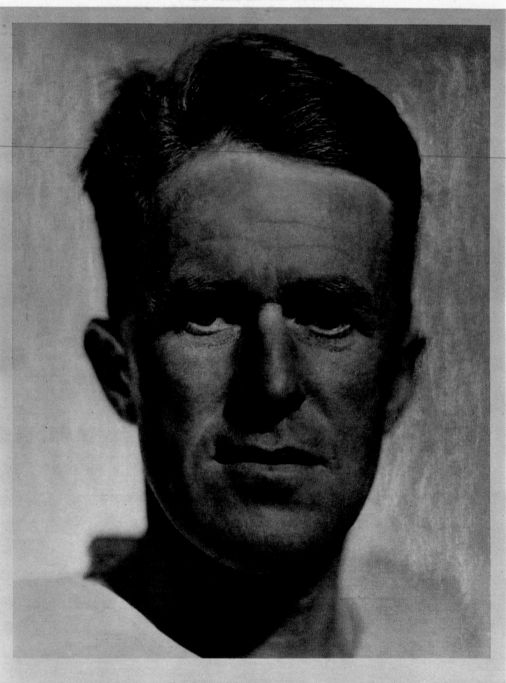

THE MOST ROMANTIC FIGURE OF THE WAR: LAWRENCE OF ARABIA.

FROM AN UNPUBLISHED CAMERA PORTRAIT BY HOWARD COSTER.

AN "ARCHÆOLOGIST-PHILOSOPHER" (IN LORD ALLENBY'S WORDS) AND "A BRILLIANT TACTICIAN, WITH A GENIUS FOR LEADERSHIP":
THE LATE COLONEL T. E. LAWRENCE (T. E. SHAW), THE MOVING SPIRIT OF THE ARAB REVOLT DURING THE WAR.

Lawrence of Arabia, the most romantic and legendary figure of the Great War, who had faced and escaped a hundred deaths during his amazing career as leader of the Arab Revolt, died at last, on May 19, from the effects of a motor-cycling accident in a Dorset lane. He was born in Wales, near Snowdon, in 1888. As an Oxford undergraduate, he wandered through many countries of the Near East, assimilating the Arab spirit and speech, and for a time he did archæological work at Carchemish. Meanwhile he had deeply studied military history and technique. Thus he was drawn into the war fully equipped for his destined task. Afterwards he was awarded a research fellowship at All Souls, and published his famous book, "The Seven Pillars of Wisdom." In 1921, as Political Adviser on the Middle East at the Colonial Office, he inspired the foundation of Arab kingdoms in Iraq and Transjordan. A year later he enlisted in the ranks of the Air Force, afterwards transferring to the Tank Corps, and formally adopting the name of Shaw. In 1925 he returned to the R.A.F., as an aircraftman, and left it only a few weeks ago to retire to his Dorset cottage in the village of Moreton. In a tribute to his memory, Lord Allenby calls him "the mainspring of the Arab movement."

Full page from the Illustrated London News announcing the death of T. E. Lawrence.

Augustus John overlooking the escort of the coffin.

send a telegram. He had checked in with his neighbor Mrs. Knowles about cooking lunch the next day for him and his visitor Henry Williamson and asked if she needed anything from the shops. Around 10:30, on his Brough Su-

perior, he headed to town, about a mile and a half away from Clouds Hill. It was a bright day but windy. At Bovington, he mailed a package of books to his friend Jock Chambers and sent off a telegram to Henry Williamson

Onlookers at the grave of T. E. Lawrence

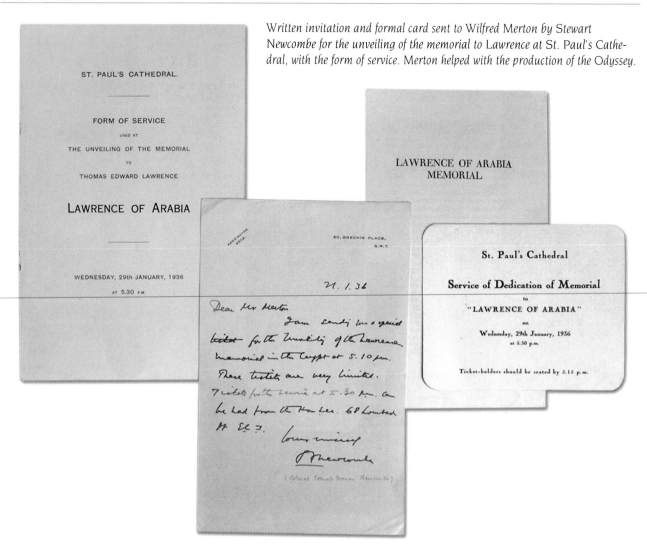

Written invitation and formal card sent to Wilfred Merton by Stewart Newcombe for the unveiling of the memorial to Lawrence at St. Paul's Cathedral, with the form of service. Merton helped with the production of the Odyssey.

stating that his planned visit tomorrow was fine, even if it rained. About 11:20 Lawrence headed back home. The road between Clouds Hill and Bovington has three dips, two deep enough to lose sight of the oncoming road. It seems that a black delivery van coming in the opposite direction caused Lawrence to move slightly to the edge of the road. After the van passed and he came over a rise, Lawrence suddenly came upon two boys on bikes riding in his direction. Swerving quickly trying to avoid them, he caught the back end of a bicycle, lost control of his motorcycle and was flung violently to the ground. Corporal Catchpole, walking his dog, heard the crash, came upon the unconscious and bloody Lawrence. He waved down a passing army truck and helped the driver take Lawrence and one of the boys to the Bovington Camp hospital.

When word reached authorities that the accident victim was Lawrence, tight control over any released information was enforced. Top doctors were called in for care and consultation. The War Office immediately started an investigation into the accident and interviewed the boys and Corporal Catchpole. Newspaper reporters began to push for more information while Lawrence remained unconscious. The King

telephoned asking to be kept informed on Lawrence's condition. He never came out of his coma. His condition worsened and he passed away on Sunday morning, May 19th.

On the morning of May 21st, an official inquest was held concerning his death. Catchpole estimated Lawrence to be going between fifty and sixty miles per hour. He reported seeing a black car. The two boys stated they pulled into single file when they heard a motorcycle coming from behind. They did not see a black car. A doctor from the Bovington hospital gave details about his head injury. The jury gave a verdict that Lawrence had died of injuries received accidentally. That didn't stop rumors and wild speculation about the accident from being raised. There was talk of Lawrence being murdered, a victim of his own government, or the Arabs, or the Zionists. The black car raised questions. Did it run Lawrence off the road? Was his death staged so he could go off and raise tribesmen in rebellion? These wild conspiracy theories dismiss the fact that Lawrence lived alone in quiet isolation and if somebody truly wanted to have him killed, could have done it in a much simpler fashion. Catchpole's testimony that Lawrence was going over fifty is dismissed by the fact that the crashed Brough was found stuck in second

Lawrence bust by Eric Kennington at St. Paul's Cathedral.

Postcard sent by Eric Kennington,
showing his medieval inspired effigy of Lawrence.

gear, used at a top speed of 38 miles per hour. The facts bear out that it was simply a tragic motorcycle accident.

While Lawrence lay unconscious, his brother Arnold realized that chances of his surviving the crash were slim. His mother and brother Robert were in China and unable to return. Arrangements were made for a simple funeral service. Some of his friends were already at Bovington out of concern for Lawrence and when he died on Sunday, the funeral was set for Tuesday afternoon. The family had asked that the public not attend. Lawrence had requested that he be buried at the small cemetery near St. Nicholas Church in Moreton, not far from Clouds Hill. The pallbearers would be friends representing different aspects of his life. The chief pallbearer was Ronald Storrs, who had accompanied Lawrence when he first visited Hussein at the start of the Arab Revolt. Eric Kennington represented the arts, having produced magnificent portraits of Lawrence and his Arabs. Corporal Bradbury of the RAF had helped

Lawrence working with the high-speed boats. Private Arthur Russell of the Tank Corps had enjoyed many evenings of classical music at Clouds Hill and remained a close friend. Stewart Newcombe represented his comrades who served with him in the Hejaz. Completing the honoured group was Pat Knowles, his neighbor from across the street.

Many of his friends came. Politicians and officers, artists, writers and privates made their way to the small church. In attendance were Churchill, Lord Lloyd, Earl Winterton, Lady Astor, A. P. Wavell, Mrs. Thomas Hardy, Bruce Rogers, Siegfried Sassoon and Augustus John. Hejaz veterans included Alan Dawnay, Brodie, Beaumont, Bailey, Rolls, Henderson, and Brown. One hymn was sung, Lawrence's favorite, "Jesu, Lover of my Soul." It was just a short walk to the cemetery. After the plain coffin was lowered into the plot, a young girl threw in a small bunch of violets. In the coffin his brother Arnold had already placed some pieces of grass from Akaba.

-Appendices-

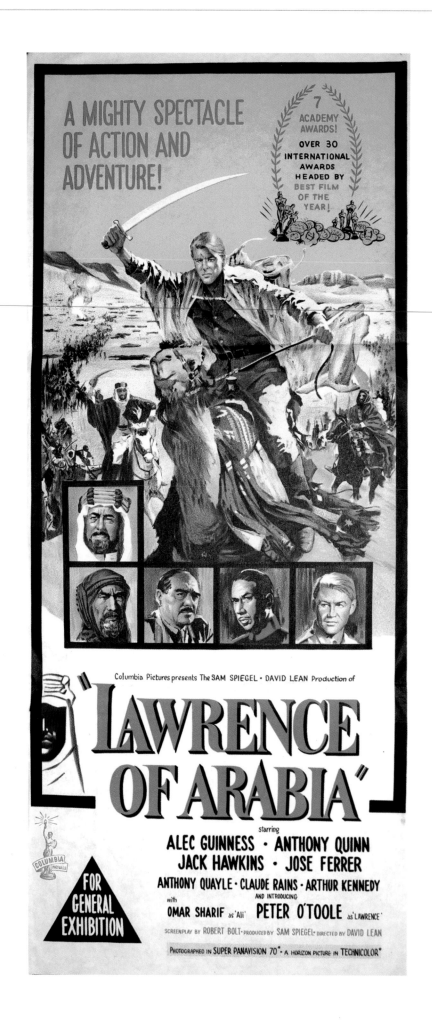

Appendix 1
-Lawrence Heritage-

T. E. Lawrence
and the film "Lawrence of Arabia"

For the generation after the First World War, it was Lowell Thomas that made Lawrence of Arabia a household name. Through his multi-media stage presentation that was seen by an estimated one million people, Thomas presented Lawrence as a modest man of action liberating the Arabs from the oppressing Turks. For the generations of the sixties, it was the David Lean film that sparked a renewed interest in Lawrence, now viewed as a hero with flaws.

Even during Lawrence's lifetime attempts were made to film his story. With the publishing of his lavishly produced book *Seven Pillars of Wisdom*, Lawrence was left with a debt of over thirteen thousand pounds. Subscriptions to the book were taken at 30 pounds each, though eventually the cost to produce one was 90 pounds. By the fall of 1926, Lawrence and his literary agent, Raymond Savage, approached the British film producer Herbert Wilcox about the possibility of making a movie based on his story. Wilcox was not sold on the idea. Though Lawrence felt it would make an outstanding film, Wilcox took a pass. Lawrence was soon able to get out of debt by abridging his book to a war story titled *Revolt in the Desert* and having Jonathon Cape publish it. It was agreed that he would only take enough royalties to clear his debt, and that any additional profit to go to the Royal Air Force Benevolent Fund. For now, he lost interest in any personal involvement with a movie being made of his Hejaz campaign.

The next major pursuit to film the Lawrence story would take place in 1934. By that time the Graves biography had been in print for several years and the Lowell Thomas book was still selling well. Joining these books was Liddell Hart's own biography of Lawrence. Raymond Savage approached Liddell Hart about doing work for a Lawrence film and the possibility of selling the film rights to his book. He sought Lawrence's advice and was a bit surprised when Lawrence did not object completely to the project, perhaps thinking with Liddell Hart's involvement, a decent film could possibly be made.

The well-known Alexander Korda would direct the film and Liddell Hart and Korda entered negotiations. Lawrence followed it all closely, even making suggestions to his friend and banker Robin Buxton about who might play his part, suggesting Walter Hudd or perhaps even Leslie Howard. Needed agreement was reached between Korda's film company, London Films, and the trustees of Lawrence's *Revolt in the Desert* fund. By January, 1935, though, with his retirement from the Royal Air Force fast approaching, Lawrence met with Korda and persuaded him to drop the film project entirely, at least as long as he was alive. He also got Korda to agree to not make a public announcement of stopping the film thus preventing someone else from picking up the idea. Raymond Savage and Liddell Hart, both of whom were planning to make money off any film deal, were disappointed. Savage even started making plans of selling the story by going around Lawrence. Liddell Hart was getting mixed signals from Lawrence and in a meeting in March, Lawrence now said he had no objection to some film deal, perhaps even working on one behind the scenes, as long as it wasn't based on his own book.

On May 19, Lawrence died. Within weeks, a flurry of activity reviving the film project had begun. Liddell Hart wanted to get involved again. Lowell Thomas wrote Korda saying any Lawrence film must have his involvement and they would have to buy rights to his book too, since he was the only reporter on the scene and it was he who first brought the story to the English public. A documentary film was quickly produced by Ace Films using many of the Lowell Thomas photographs and motion picture film. Thomas objected strongly. He accused the maker of stealing his material and threatened legal action, effectively killing this project.

With the renewed Korda project, other Lawrence friends soon got involved. Robert Graves was hired to help with dialogue, Siegfried Sassoon was added to assist and Colonel Stirling, a veteran of the Hejaz campaign who fought alongside Lawrence, would serve as technical and military advisor. Liddell Hart found himself left out and was angry about it. He threatened legal action but Korda kept him out. By 1936, a script was approved by the *Revolt in the Desert* trustees and filming was planned. The political landscape

Inspired by Lawrence's own photographs, this scene from Lawrence of Arabia featuring Peter O'Toole, Omar Sharif and Anthony Quinn was filmed in Wadi Rumm.

was changing quickly. Palestine was in growing turmoil. The relationship between Britain and Turkey was of great importance. The Foreign Office objected to any scenes that might offend the Turks. Korda sold the rights and bought them back just months later. Leslie Howard was announced to play Lawrence. Planned filming shifted from Transjordan to Egypt. By 1939, Korda was again going ahead, promising a film that would portray the Turks as heroic as possible. The start of the World War II ended Korda's plans for this film.

In 1954, Liddell Hart would become involved once again. He was hired by producer Anatole de Grunwald to be an advisor on a new Lawrence project. Playwright and screenwriter Terence Rattigan was hired to write a film based on Liddell Hart's book. The next year *The Mint* was published, as well as Richard Aldington's controversial biography of Lawrence. Plans went ahead and by 1957 Rattigan had finished his script. Dirk Bogarde was to be cast as Lawrence. By the spring of 1958, this project was abruptly called off. It was too expensive. Rattigan took his work and adapted it into a screenplay calling it *Ross*. By 1960 it was on stage in London starring Alec Guinness. Liddell Hart reached a fi-

nancial arrangement with Rattigan, agreeing that his book was the source of the Rattigan's play.

Meanwhile, A. W. Lawrence came to an agreement with Sam Spiegel, who purchased the film rights to *Seven Pillars of Wisdom*. Spiegel announced that the part of Lawrence would be played by Marlon Brando. Herbert Wilcox reentered the scene when he purchased the film rights from Rattigan for his play *Ross*. There were now dueling Lawrence film projects. Spiegel, with legal assistance, would later buy Wilcox out. With Brando delayed with the filming of *Mutiny on the Bounty*, Albert Finney tested for the role. David Lean, the film's director, did not approve. Lean, having seen Peter O'Toole in *The Day They Robbed The Bank of England* wanted him to test for the role. Lean stopped O'Toole's test early, knowing he had found his Lawrence. Arrangements were made for Robert Bolt to work on the script and by November 1960, David Lean was in Jordan scouting locations. The movie would be shot in Jordan, Spain, Morocco and England. The world premiere took place in London, December 10, 1962. Six days later, it opened in New York. Nominated for ten Academy Awards, it won seven, including Best Picture of the Year.

Many friends of Lawrence were not pleased with the film's portrayal of him. His brother, A. W. Lawrence, had already taken back permission to use the title of *Seven Pillars of Wisdom* for the film. After its release he stated in an interview that while he admired the film's spectacle, directing and music, he was bothered by his brother's portrayal, particularly of his being sadistic. *"I don't want to give the impression that I consider the Lawrence of the film to be entirely untrue. So far especially as determination, courage, and endurance are concerned, he is comparable... with the man (Mr. O'Toole) purports to represent. ...I need only say that I should not have recognized my brother."* Lowell Thomas sent A.W. letters of support and wrote his own criticism to the movie, namely its lack of historical accuracy, and he praised only the camels. Liddell Hart wrote letters protesting the sadistic depiction of Lawrence at Tafas. This was not the Lawrence he knew.

The movie did find a receptive public, however, willing to take a longer look at a flawed hero. More biographies appeared and even the Lowell Thomas book *With Lawrence in Arabia* was reprinted, with a still from the movie on the cover.

With much fanfare a restored version of the film was released in 1989. The acclaimed effort of Robert Harris rescued the film and David Lean offered a Director's cut. By now the accuracy of the film was second to the cinematic masterpiece that it was. That same year the National Portrait Gallery in London staged a blockbuster show on Lawrence. It offered a real glimpse of Lawrence, featuring artifacts from all periods of his life. It also benefitted from the latest research from the archives that supported Lawrence's own writings and outstanding achievements. It provided the perfect balance of the man, the real life versus the reel one.

Omar Sharif was disappointed that an Arab actor was not chosen for the role of Auda abu Tayi. Anthony Quinn however put in a memorable performance.

Arthur Kennedy as the war correspondent Jackson Bentley,
Lowell Thomas was upset about his character Jackson Bentley and like A. W. Lawrence was quite critical of the film.

There have been several noteworthy documentaries made on Lawrence's life. In 1962, Malcolm Brown and the BBC produced one that included many interviews of the important people who knew Lawrence including Lowell Thomas, war colleagues Alec Kirkbride and S. C. Rolls, and his commander at Mount Batten, Wing Commander Sydney Smith and his wife Clare. Parts of this documentary were used in a 1986 production by Julia Cave and Malcolm Brown, with additional interviews of A. W. Lawrence and Arthur Russell. Noted Arab writers Edward Said and Suleiman Mousa also give their judgments on Lawrence's achievements.

Lawrence's involvement at the Versailles Peace Conference is examined in the made-for-television drama A *Dangerous Man* starring Ralph Fiennes as Lawrence. Most recently is the PBS-backed *Lawrence of Arabia, The Battle for the Arab World*. Written, produced and directed by James Hawes, it uses archival footage and reenactments to present Lawrence and the Arab Revolt.

Researching Lawrence

Doing first hand research into any subject is an exciting opportunity. With Lawrence, there are several main venues available. While there may be little surprises to be found directly related to Lawrence, there is much available material

to research that supplements what we know about the Arab Revolt and the many other participants who fought in it.

Internet research.

Most major research collections have an Internet component. Here are some very worthwhile collections available through the Internet.

The Australian War Memorial. This site has a database of thousands of photographs and artifacts. It is searchable by word. Included are numerous photos of the Imperial Camel Corps and the Australian Flying Corps. Artifacts in the collection include a robe and headdress of Lawrence, the medals of Ross Smith, Turkish flags and uniforms, many Lighthorse items and a Hejaz flag. This museum organized a major show on Lawrence and the Lighthorse and the catalogue of that exhibition is online with many photographs of the displays and artifacts illustrated.

The American Colony of Jerusalem photographs are in the collection of the **Library of Congress.** Its database is searchable and the photographs are out of copyright. Photos include hundreds taken during the Turkish occupation of Jerusalem, with many shots of soldiers and important officials. Lawrence is represented in the collection with photos of his post-war visits to Palestine and Transjordan.

The Lowell Thomas Papers at **Marist College**. This website of the Lowell Thomas archives includes hundreds of images taken by Harry Chase in Egypt, Palestine and the Hejaz including his well known photographs of Lawrence. The travel diaries and lecture notes of Lowell Thomas are also available online.

The T. E. Lawrence Studies website maintained by Jeremy Wilson is an expanding research tool that includes biographical details and many photographs. Plans are to include hundreds of archival documents on the website, making research using original sources even easier.

The T. E. Lawrence Society website is updated with the latest symposium information, held every other year. Access to Society newsletters and journals are limited to members.

Public collections

The National Archives in Kew Gardens, England, is available for researchers. Visitors must register for a reader's card and pass a test on how to safely use original documents. In this collection are army records, the official logs of the Hejaz Armoured Car Battery, the Royal

Flying Corps Hejaz detachments, and papers of the Arab Bureau. Recently, the National Archives has allowed researchers to take digital photographs of documents. In time, this should allow many of these original documents to be posted on-line to make them available to all and to avoid the potential damage caused by handling the original documents.

The Imperial War Museum, Research Room and Photograph Archive. An appointment is needed for use. The photo archive has hundreds of photos of the Arab Revolt, many taken and donated by Lawrence. Photographs can be ordered and a photocopier is available if you want a reference shot. A limited number of photographs are listed online. The library contains papers of Peake, Garland, and others. An online catalog is available. Photocopies can be ordered.

Private Institutions.

The following institutions have the largest Lawrence holdings of original material. Access is limited. You have to apply for access, with references, to obtain a reader's card. Use of the material is limited with approval. In most cases, copies of letters and documents can be obtained for research purposes. Use of a digital camera is permitted, under their guidelines.

Bodleian Library, Oxford. This collection holds a massive amount of original Lawrence material, most of it donated

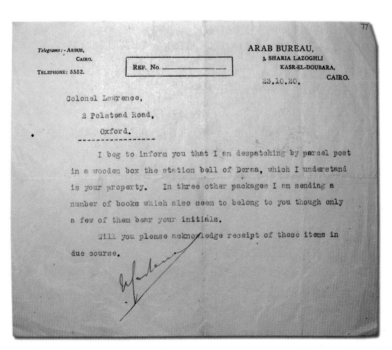

Letter from Bimbashi Garland of the Arab Bureau informing Lawrence that some parcels of books and the railway station bell of Deraa is heading his way. Robert Graves notes that Lawrence would ring a station bell while at All Souls. This letter gives us good evidence that he indeed had a station bell. Bodleian Library Collection, Oxford.

by Lawrence and his family. The catalogue is available online. The unedited versions of Lawrence's letters that were assembled by David Garnett can be found here. The original Hejaz photographs by Lawrence published in *Oriental Assembly* are here also.

Harry Ransom Center, University of Texas at Austin. A large collection of original letters, manuscripts, photographs and artwork by and related to Lawrence. Much of this collection was obtained directly from Liddell Hart. The catalogue is available online.

Edwards Metcalf Collection of T. E. Lawrence, Huntington Library, San Marino, California. This collection, put together by well-known Lawrence collector Edwards Metcalf, includes many original Lawrence letters and manuscripts and almost every variation of Lawrence book published before 1980. The catalogue is available online.

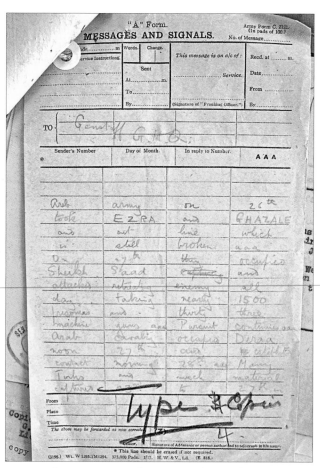

Original message written by Lawrence during the advance on Damascus, to General Headquarters of the E.E.F. National Archives, Kew.

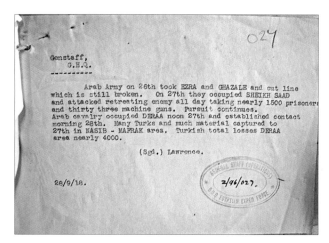

Typed copy of Lawrence's message for General Headquarters. National Archives, Kew.

Typed copy of Buxton's telegram detailing the capture of Mudawara Station of the Hejaz Railway. National Archives, Kew.

Arab jambiya given by Lawrence to Buxton. In the drawing of lots between Buxton's Camel Corps officers, Douglas Peerman won the dagger. Edwards Metcalf Collection, Huntington Library.

Collecting Lawrence

Lawrence realized even in his lifetime that items associated with him would be of value. He even encouraged some friends who had an original edition of *Seven Pillars of Wisdom* to sell it if the money was good. Collectors eagerly sought autographed letters of Lawrence. Lawrence seemed to ignore "fan mail" and was aware of this market. After his death though, a number of his friends began selling their Lawrence material. Robert Graves sold a mass of correspondence he had from Lawrence, mostly put together while he was working on his Lawrence biography.

Likely on the top of most Lawrence collector's lists is a copy of the 1926 *Seven Pillars of Wisdom*. Surprisingly, almost every year there are one or two copies for sale, mostly through the higher end auction houses. Some collectors want the "Complete Issue", while others might seek out an "Incomplete Issue", sometimes more interesting because Lawrence usually presented these copies to friends, often with inscriptions.

Most of us aren't in the league to spend the money for an original *Seven Pillars of Wisdom*. Next best might be a Lawrence letter. Some experts think Lawrence wrote over four thousand letters in his lifetime. Many have been catalogued and their contents published. Some autograph collectors find it more interesting to have an unpublished letter. I have known some collectors who will refuse to let the contents be published and guard them rather secretly. However, there are others that take delight in pointing out that they own a certain published letter. Prices for letters vary greatly depending on the content and whom the letter may be addressed. You may be able to find a letter for 1000 pounds but others have been auctioned recently for over ten times that amount. Lawrence signed his name T. E. Lawrence, J.M. Ross and T.E. Shaw. There are collectors that seek out examples of each signature, though most of the Ross signatures are on his bank cheques and not letters. In 1923, Lawrence enlisted into the R.A.F. using the alias "T. E. Shaw" eventually changing his name officially to Shaw. Letters dating from this period and on are signed Shaw, not

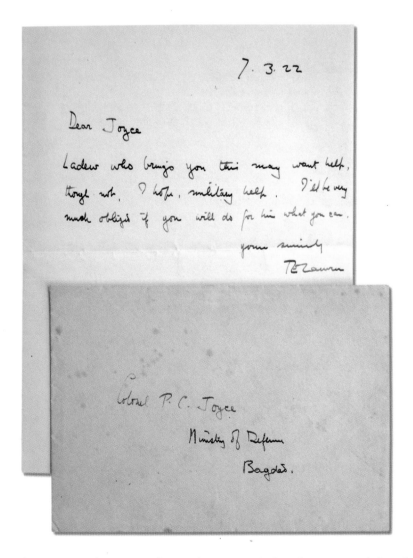

Letter of introduction written by Lawrence for American Harvey Ladew who was to travel through Iraq.
His companion, Alexander Powell, would write about their adventures in the book By Car and Camel to the Peacock Throne.

A rare signed photograph of Lawrence.
Photograph taken by George Lloyd, October 1917.

offered over the years. Nuri as-Said is easier to locate because he had such a long political career in Iraq.

Book collectors will find much to collect with Lawrence. A nice addition to any collection is a book from the Lawrence library at Clouds Hill. When Lawrence died, his brother inventoried the book collection and this list was published in T. E. *Lawrence by His Friends*. This is by no means a complete list of Lawrence books. His brother Arnold would occasionally sell copies in his possession that were Lawrence's books but were not on the list. Lawrence also gave many books away during his lifetime and these occasionally come on the market. The books from Clouds Hill should have the proper Clouds Hill bookplate pasted in. These were made up after Lawrence's death and placed in the book prior to the break up of his library. Collectors should take some caution though. There were some extra bookplates made up and there seems to be some debate on how many of these labels may have made it into the market. Some of Lawrence's books were cheap editions and a common 5 pound book becomes a five hundred pound book with the addition of the Clouds Hill bookplate. Also, fake bookplates have been made, though there are some slight differences between the fake ones and the real ones. If you want a Clouds Hill book, the best bet is to get an author's inscribed copy or numbered copy presented to Lawrence, so you have sure proof authenticity. A reputable book dealer familiar with Lawrence material is your best guide for Clouds Hill books.

Many of the men around Lawrence wrote books. A collector can build up a nice group of books written by Lawrence's favorite authors and some signed copies are available at reasonable prices. Sassoon and Garnett published signed, limited editions. My collection favors the military, not just the literary, and I've found books signed by Peake, Stirling, Kirkbride, Storrs, Winterton and Young. Signed copies of the Lowell Thomas biography can be found at reasonable

Lawrence. He would also signed many of his letters just using his initials.

Autographed letters and signatures of Lawrence's friends and military peers can make a fascinating collection. I've been putting together a set of letters and signatures to go with the *Seven Pillars of Wisdom* illustrations. Examples of Allenby and Storrs are easy to find. Harder to obtain are the lesser military figures like Joyce and Young. The Arabs are most difficult to get, though I've seen some Feisal letters

An uncommon version of Lawrence's signature, signed J. H. Ross. He kept the Ross signature on his bank account, even after he changed his name officially to Thomas Edward Shaw in 1927. This cheque, made out to Eric Kennington, was most likely for payment related to his work on Seven Pillars of Wisdom.

Close up of an authentic Clouds Hill bookplate.

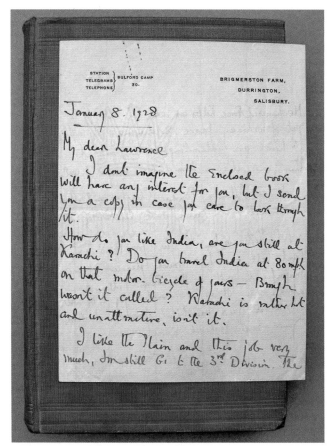

Letter from General Wavell to Lawrence presenting him with a copy of his book The Palestine Campaigns. Lawrence kept a surprising number of letters from his correspondents.

prices too. Book collecting is much easier now with the computer based inventories like ABE books. I have found hard to find titles I thought I would never get. Some collectors are particular about dust jackets and true first editions. Phil O'Brien's excellent bibliography on Lawrence is a must have reference for the Lawrence book collector.

Examples of the Hejaz stamps that Lawrence helped design are available for a few pounds. Expect to pay much more though for a wartime used cover bearing the stamps. I have seen two covers sent by Lawrence himself that would be a true gem in any collection.

Lawrence had a personal disdain for medals. However medals to men who served with Lawrence occasionally make it to the market and are highly collectable and get very high prices. World War I British medals are named to the recipient so you can be certain of their authenticity. One can research the man through the records at the National Archives. It is much easier to find the medals to a man who served in Palestine with Allenby than it is to get a set of medals to a man who served with Lawrence in the Hejaz. Medals to men of the Imperial Camel Corps do come up for sale but you need to remember that not all men in the Camel Corps served with Lawrence in the Hejaz. Research is key.

There are many Lawrence-related items that can be found for a reasonable amount of money. Recently I saw a postcard collection put together with a Lawrence theme. The collector had bought postcards from Oxford of the time Lawrence lived there. He added postcards of Egypt from places associated with Lawrence like the Savoy Hotel and the Continental Hotel. He found postcards of the many ships that assisted Lawrence and the Arab Revolt. He added postcards of Clouds Hill, published soon after it was given to the National Trust. It was a truly exceptional collection, put together for not too much money, with items found mostly on eBay.

A word about fakes. If there is a market for it, there will

be fakes. There are plenty of Lawrence fakes to be aware of and more being made. Again knowledge is your best key. Lawrence signed a copy of *Revolt in the Desert* for Charlotte Shaw. He refused to sign any others. He even sent copies back to friends, not signed, but included a letter explaining why he refused to sign the book. That said, almost every year brings a reputed signed copy of *Revolt in the Desert*. They are fakes, despite what the seller says.

I've seen several Lawrence daggers for sale. We know Lawrence had three daggers. There are photos of Lawrence wearing each one. The earliest dagger was traded away to a Howeitat chief, the smaller gold one is at All Souls and the last one is in a private English collection. That said, a major London auction house recently sold a Moroccan dagger once owned by Lawrence. It was given to a mechanic of George Brough who had gotten to know Lawrence by doing repairs to his motorcycles. The provenance was good and Lawrence might have even owned the dagger, but it was misleading to give the impression that this dagger was one used by him in the Hejaz. Be very cautious when the item's description says, *"Stated by vendor to be."* You are taking the word of the seller that the item is what the vendor says it is. You need to feel sure

Frederick Peake's full dress tunic of the Arab Legion. Occasionally uniforms to officers who served with Lawrence will come up for sale. Provenance is extremely important with these items.

William Marshall's full dress tunic, pouch and belts of the Royal Army Medical Corps.

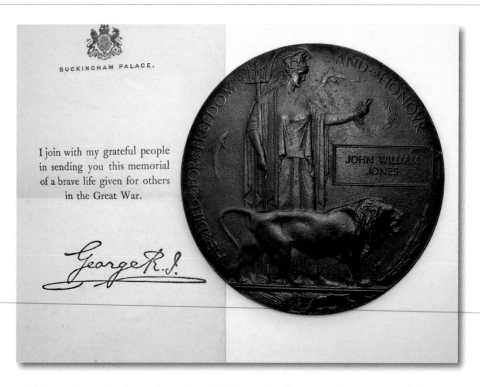

Named medals to British participants in the Arab Revolt are highly sought after. British WWI war medals were individually named. This named Memorial Plaque, in addition to his war medals, was presented to the family of John William Jones, the Imperial Camel Corps officer killed during the attack on Mudawara Station.

MODEL OF THE *GOLDEN HIND*

Built by Sydney and T. E. S. in their spare time. The hull was made by T. E. S. himself.

Photograph of the model of the Golden Hind made by Sydney Smith and Lawrence.

The Golden Hind before restoration. The ship was previously owned by noted Lawrence collector and biographer Robert Payne. Edwards Metcalf obtained it when the Payne collection was sold.

about the provenance of the item. A pair of military issue WWI binoculars will sell for about 50 pounds but I've seen two pairs sold that had T.E.L. engraved on them and supposedly belonged to him. While the larger auction houses are pretty cautious about what they sell, they too can also make mistakes. A case in point is the doubted authenticity of a Lawrence watch and cigarette case. The sale was withdrawn.

Some of the best things come on the market when a major collection is being put up for auction. The noted collection of Bruce Tovee came to auction soon after his death. The collection of Robert Payne had many outstanding items. Peter Hopkirk's collection, including many fine books and Lawrence's Arabic dictionary, was sold at auction. The Spiro Collection including notable editions of the 1926 *Seven Pillars* and many interesting letters was sold at Christie's. The auction catalogues to these larger sales are great reference tools for any Lawrence collector. Some of the smaller country auction houses will sell the less expensive items with the rare, big ticket items sent to London. When Joyce Knowles died, many interesting Lawrence-associated items came to market through a smaller auction house.

There are great *"right and correct"* Lawrence-related items that come up for sale every year, but there are also fakes. Working with a known dealer that stands by what he sells

will help. I bought a typed, signed Lawrence letter from a reputable book dealer specializing in Churchill. When I got the letter in hand and did more research on it, I realized it was a fake. The original letter was in the Bodleian and it was hand written. Pointing this out to the dealer, he took it back and withdrew it from his listing. Any collector will encounter fakes. It's part of the education you earn. But it can be a costly education. Don't let your own mind talk you into something being right. Provenance is extremely important.

You will find interesting and hard to find items on eBay, but be very cautious about the objects that have any first hand Lawrence connection. Looking on eBay is good for the small pieces of ephemera; the postcard, the Hejaz cover, the Lowell Thomas program, the WWI map of Sinai, all fantastic items that before eBay you might have stumbled on in the corner of a book shop. Finding good collectable Lawrence items has never been easier, but I miss so many of those book shops.

Tracking T. E. Lawrence Today
London:

A visitor on a quick trip to London can see some worthwhile places with a Lawrence connection. One should visit 14 Barton Street, located a short walk from Westminster Abby. It's a small street and you won't find it on the free maps of London. The house is marked by one of the famous blue plaques. It was in the attic room that Lawrence spent long hours working on the draft of the *Seven Pillars of Wisdom*, from late 1919 to 1923. Sir Herbert Baker, a well-known architect, had his offices here and let Lawrence use the attic. Lawrence felt Baker's staff did a commendable job protecting his privacy. Lawrence told Baker it was *"the best-and-freest place I have ever lived in, nobody has found me...despite efforts by callers and telephones."*

The Imperial War Museum has a special connection with Lawrence. Charles ffoulkes, its first curator, was one of Lawrence's friends. After the war, Lawrence gave the Imperial War Museum many objects including the wreath from Saladin's tomb. His family presented additional robes and an Arab headdress. Lawrence's rifle is on display, a gift from King George V. The museum features a large display case highlighting exhibits from Lawrence and the Hejaz campaign. On exhibit have been the medals of Allenby, Joyce and Junor, the Derwent Wood bust of Lawrence, a flag of the Hejaz, and a gift rifle from Feisal to Boyle. Various camel saddles and weapons are also displayed. The photo library houses a large collection of Hejaz war photographs including many made from Lawrence's own negatives, but an appointment must be made to look at these.

St. Paul's Cathedral has a memorial to Lawrence of Arabia. Soon after his death, a solicitation by his friends to raise money for a memorial took place. The memorial at St. Paul's is located in the crypt and features the Kennington bust of Lawrence. It was dedicated on January 29, 1936, with music Lawrence was fond of and an address by Viscount Halifax. The service concluded with Reveille by the trumpeters of the Royal Air Force.

Along the Thames Embankment is the monument to the men of the Imperial Camel Corps. This memorial lists the names of all those killed who had served in the Imperial Camel Corps including the ones lost in the capture of the Mudawara railway station. The dedication in July 1921 was attended by Chetwode, Smith V.C., Winterton, Buxton, and many members of the Camel Corps.

Lawrence Memorial
at St. Paul's Cathedral, London.

Lawrence rented to top floor from architect Herbert Baker
to work on Seven Pillars of Wisdom. 14 Barton Street, London.

Oxford:

There are a number of important places in Oxford to visit associated with Lawrence. For the visitor, Oxford is easily reached by bus or train from London. The service is very regular and a return and back the same day is very easy to do.

The Lawrence family home is located at 2 Polstead Road. This is a private residence, so please respect that. One can still get a sense of the neighborhood in which Lawrence and his brothers grew up and from this house the boys would bicycle to the City of Oxford High

School. In the back yard, one can see the small two-room bungalow built for young T. E., giving him more privacy and independence.

The Ashmolean Museum has many connections with Lawrence. His mentor, D. G. Hogarth, was Keeper at the Ashmolean. Lawrence presented the museum his portrait of Hogarth by Augustus John. The collection houses many of the small objects collected by Lawrence in his early travels. Recently reinstalled and magnificently displayed are the two carved wooden Jidda doors. Also now on full view is the set of Arab garments presented to Lawrence by Feisal.

Lawrence entered Jesus College in October 1907. He did stay on campus his first term but then received special permission to live at home. With prior arrangement, you might be shown his stairway, which includes a brass rubbing made by Lawrence. The dining hall has a copy of the Augustus John portrait of Lawrence. The chapel entrance, which you can enter, has a Lawrence bust by Kennington.

All Souls College was the site of Lawrence's Fellowship given to him in 1919. He had a room here near the entrance. The College collection includes a Lawrence dagger, headdress and silver plate service, and a Kennington pastel portrait of Lawrence, though these items are not on public view.

There are other places to visit too, the Lawrence's church, St. Aldates, retains much the flavor it had during his day. St. John's College, where his brother Will attended, has his name on a memorial wall. The City of Oxford High School has rededicated a memorial plaque to Lawrence that Eric Kennington designed. It was originally unveiled by Churchill in 1936.

Imperial Camel Corps Monument, London.

2 Polstead Road, Oxford.

Dorset:

In 1923, Lawrence joined the Royal Tank Corps and was stationed at Bovington, Dorset. He rented a small cottage nearby called Clouds Hill and would make it his home until his death in 1935. A day in the countryside of Dorset visiting Clouds Hill and nearby Lawrence sites is a must for any enthusiast.

Bovington and its Tank Museum can be reached by train out of London to Wool. From the station it is 1 ¾ miles to the Tank Museum. It's a pleasant walk but there are usually cabs available for hire. The Tank Museum has a display of Lawrence artifacts from men who served with him in the Hejaz. This group of items has shifted locations recently during the remodeling. The collection holds items from several armoured car soldiers and loaned items from Captain Siddons, a pilot from "X flight."

Also on display is a 1920 model Rolls Royce armoured car. This model differs just slightly from the 1914 model used by Lawrence. The wheels on the earlier version would be spoked wheels, like those found on a heavy-duty bicycle. Lawrence's cars would be a tan colour, not green, but this 1920 model gives you a great impression on what they were like.

From the Tank Museum, it is 2 ½ miles to Clouds Hill. There is a hiking guide available if you would like to walk. Clouds Hill is open from mid-March until the end of Oc-

Jesus College, Oxford.

Clouds Hill,

City of Oxford High School, Oxford.

Lawrence's grave at Moreton.
His mother and elder brother selected the religious inscription. At the foot of the grave are the words Dominus illuminatio mea, the opening words of Psalm 27 meaning the The Lord is my light. Carved on an open book, it is the emblem and motto of Oxford University.

tober. The National Trust has built a new reception area and gift shop near by. The small house still retains the charm and secluded isolation that Lawrence so wanted. Plans are underway to restore the downstairs bookroom with volumes similar to the ones Lawrence kept there. The original library was sold off years ago by the family. Most of the furniture and fixtures are original. Lawrence designed the reading chair and some of the fixtures himself. Down the road to Bovington is the site of Lawrence's fatal accident.

Near Clouds Hill is Moreton, 1 ¾ miles away. Lawrence's funeral took place at St. Nicholas Church in Moreton. The church was heavily damaged by a bomb during WW II and its windows rebuilt honoring the Royal Air Force. Near the church is the cemetery where Lawrence is buried.

The nearby town of Wareham has some Lawrence sites. There is a tourist information office that will provide you with a leaflet. The Town Museum has a small number of items associated with Lawrence. The Anglebury Coffee House and Tea Rooms will show you the window seat

used by Lawrence. At St. Martin's Church, the oldest church in Dorset dating to 1030 rests the stone effigy of Lawrence sculpted by Eric Kennington.

A day spent in Lawrence's Dorset is very rewarding. However, Clouds Hill and the cemetery are a bit off the path. If you don't have a car, your day will be made much easier arranging pick up times with taxi drivers ahead of time.

Arab Revolt Archaeology in Jordan Today

A team of English archaeologists are working with Jordanian authorities to document, survey and catalogue various sites associated with the Arab Revolt's fight against the Ottoman Empire during the First World War. Until recently, very little fieldwork had been done to preserve important Jordanian locations associated with the Arab Revolt. Though there has been active research on the ancient sites of Jordan, little progress has been made preserving any of the modern sites in the country.

Since 2005, Dr. Neil Faulkner has led a team called The Great Arab Revolt Project (GARP) to investigate the remains of the First World War in Jordan. GARP, with

Hejaz Railway bridge north of Mudawara.

Damaged railway buildings at Wadi Rutm.

GARP *volunteers at work excavating Turkish tent rings.*

Looking south to Tell Shahm.

the cooperation of HRH Prince Hassan, the Jordanian Department of Antiquities, and the Council for British Research in the Levant, is a ten-year project with a goal to document and preserve important Arab Revolt sites. The GARP team is working to catalogue railway stations, trench works, forts, and army bases used during the 1914-1918 war. The Jordanian government recognizes the vital role the Revolt played in its history and realizes the potential for tourist visits to these heritage sites.

A team of volunteers working with GARP archaeologists has already documented ruined Hejaz railway stations, former Turkish forts, surviving Ottoman trenches, as well as the site of the Arab attack at Aba el Lissan.

By comparing reconnaissance photographs taken during the war with aerial images from Google Earth, amazing discoveries have been made. The GARP team was surprised how extensive the Turkish trenches were around Ma'an. Modern technology has allowed team members to walk and plot the existing trench systems using a GPS (global positioning system) receiver set to record its location every second. This data is then transferred into a computer software program to produce a map of the trench system.

Metal detectors are used to scan battle sites in order to locate and record the various bullet casings found. The metal detectorists can then grid out their findings and determine incoming and outgoing fire by examining the different types of bullets used. How many bullets found along a firing line can determine what a battle looked like over ninety years ago. Established Turkish tent areas have been excavated as well, resulting in the discovery of tunic buttons, remains of food cans, a patch of Turkish army uniform, and even an officer's document seal.

The project has led a team into Jordan every fall for the digging season. The Great Arab Revolt Project is based at the University of Bristol and maintains a website with the latest information about their accomplishments and upcoming fieldwork. Their work in conflict archeology is to be commended. The first phase of the ten-year project was concentrated on sites between Ma'an and Mudawara. The second five year phase will center on the area between Ma'an and Akaba. This area was contested strongly by Ottoman forces against the Arab armies, both regular and irregular, and British forces.

The Great Arab Revolt Project's fieldwork is leading to a better understanding of the day-to-day life of the soldier on campaign. It is also drawing attention to the need to preserve many of these physical sites of the Arab Revolt that have been neglected by time, recognizing the important role they played in Jordanian history and the shaping of the modern Middle East.

Lawrence at Hejaz bridge, 1918

Appendix 2
-Stamps of the Hejaz-

A SHORT NOTE on the DESIGN and ISSUE of POSTAGE STAMPS Prepared by the ⚘ ⚘ SURVEY of EGYPT for HIS HIGHNESS ⚘ HUSEIN ⚘ ⚘ ⚘ Emir & Sherif of Mecca & KING of the HEJAZ

El-Qahira, MCMXVIII

After Sherif Hussein of Mecca declared the Arab Revolt, there needed to be a new symbol of nationhood; postage stamps. The story of the development and production of these stamps for this emerging nation is an interesting one. It was felt that the new stamps should be uniquely Arab in design. The Survey of Egypt, under the Director-General Mr. Ernest M Dawson, and the maker of military maps, would produce the stamps. Ronald Storrs, the Oriental Secretary of Egypt and later the Military Governor of Jerusalem, and Lawrence took charge of the project. Storrs sent his feelings to Hussein stating that the stamps would be *"an entirely new and independent national issue"* and that the *"design should in wording, spirit, and ornament be, as far as possible, representative of a purely Arab source and inspiration."* Storrs and Lawrence found examples of Islamic designs in and around Cairo and modified them for the stamps. Inspiration for the designs came from a Koran page, a detail of a carved Koran page from a sultan's tomb, a carved panel door from a mosque, and detail work from a prayer niche. Lawrence even looked into the possibility of using different flavored gums for the issues, an idea that was ultimately rejected.

The stamp designs were approved by Sherif Hussein and by August 1916, the first issues were in production.

More values and postage due stamps were soon added. Lawrence took to this task quite enthusiastically. Storrs writes *"it was quickly apparent that Lawrence already possessed or had quickly assimilated a complete working technique of philatelic and three-colour reproduction, so he was able to supervise the issue from start to finish."* Lawrence's letters to his family kept them up to date on the trails of stamp production. He even sent examples of the latest issues to his younger brother Arnold. Sheets of 50 were delivered to the noted stamp collector, King George V.

After the war, The Survey of Egypt published a limited edition book describing in great detail the various states, proofs and roulette issues of the stamps. Two hundred numbered copies were printed and presented to those involved with the production, with some additional copies sent to museums and libraries. The Imperial War Museum has a copy. Lawrence's own dedicated copy was sold recently. By November 1918, in the service newspaper The Palestine News, stamp dealers were already placing want ads to purchase postally used examples of the Hejaz stamps. Even today, war covers of the Hejaz are hard to find, the most sought-after examples being covers addressed by Lawrence himself. The Hejaz issues can be found in modern stamp catalogues listed under Saudi Arabia.

Cover with 1 piastre stamp sent by Lawrence to Ormsby-Gore of the Arab Bureau, posted from Jidda October 16, 1916.

Cover with 1/4 piastre, 1/8 piastre and 1 para addressed to Colonel Wilson at Jidda.

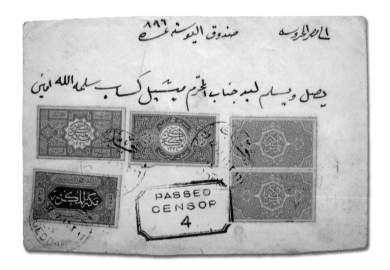

Cover with 1/8, ¼, ½ and 1 piastre stamps posted from Jidda with censor stamp.

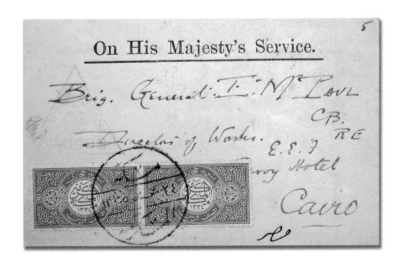

Official Government cover with ½ piastre stamps with censor stamp.

Al Nahda with Brilliants awarded to Allenby.

Hejaz Order of Al Nahda.
King Hussein created this order in October 1918 to commemorate the Arab Revolt.
It was issued to participants who made a significant contribution to the revolt.
The flag of the Hejaz is represented on the order and on the presentation box.
The sash of the First Class is also patterned after the flag.

Appendix 3
-Hejaz Orders and Medals-

The Kingdom of the Hejaz issued a series of orders and medals to present to active participants of the Arab Revolt or to significant individuals who helped the cause.

The first order founded by Sherif Hussein and the most important is the Order of Renaissance or Al Nahda. The initial distribution of this order was made on October 15th, 1918. Over the next several years, approximately 120 awards would be made to British participants in the Arab Revolt. General Allenby was awarded the highest award class, the First Class with Brilliants. Amongst the next level of First Class are Sir A. H. MacMahon, the former High Commissioner of Egypt and Sir F. R. Wingate, the former Governor General of the Sudan. Other officers awarded the

Second Class include Clayton, Dawnay, Joyce, Newcombe, and Stirling. Included in the awards for Third Class are Garland, Hornby, Marshall, Snagge, Winterton and Young. The Fourth Class ranks include the lieutenants of the armoured cars and of the Royal Air Force contingent that assisted in the Revolt. Those listed are Brodie, Gilman, Grisenthwaite and Wade of the Hejaz Armoured Car Battery and Henderson, Siddons, Stent and Smith of the Royal Air Force. The list serves has a reminder of the many British officers who assisted in a wide variety of roles during the Arab Revolt.

The Sherif asked for assistance from C. E. Wilson and P. C. Joyce in putting a list of men together to be awarded. The Arab Bureau gave notification to the British officers and distributed the award. Lawrence was to be awarded the Second Class of the Order. Notification of his award was announced in the official Hejaz government publication Al Qibla, but Lawrence never was sent the order, never made an official request to wear the order, and

Feisal is photographed wearing the Ma'an Medal and Independence Medal. Feisal presented this photograph to the visiting American archaeologist James Henry Breasted during his visit to Syria, May 1920.

Order of Al Nahda, Fourth Class, with bestowal document and presentation box awarded to Captain F. R. McKibban of the Royal Army Medical Corps. McKibban was one of several doctors to serve with Lawrence and the Hejaz army based at Akaba. Just over one hundred awards were given to British officers who played an active role in the Arab Revolt.

no announcement of his award was ever made in the official *London Gazette*. While Lawrence has a personal disdain for his own orders and medals, he did recognize their importance to his many military friends. There is correspondence from Lawrence successfully getting the Al Nahda awarded to Snagge, the naval commander at Akaba. Lawrence made additional recommendations for British gallantry awards for his fellow officers and men as well.

The Order of Independence or Istiqlal was founded in 1919. This was awarded to people who may not have participated directly in the Arab Revolt but did make significant contributions to the Kingdom.

The two medals issued by the Hejaz were the Independence Medal and the Ma'an Medal. The Independence Medal was first issued by 1920. This commemorates the proclamation of independence in 1916.

The Ma'an Medal commemorates that fighting which took place in the Ma'an area in April of 1918. The medal was officially announced in November 1919. Over five hundred medals were awarded to Arab participants.

The Kingdom of the Hejaz was short-lived. By 1926, Abdul Aziz had taken over the territory and was proclaimed King of the Hejaz and the Sultan of Nejd. In 1932, the Kingdom of Saudi Arabia was proclaimed.

The two original Hejaz orders of Al Nahda and Istiqlal were modified slightly and continue to be issued by the Kingdom of Jordan.

Ma'an Medal and Independence Medal. Ma'an Medal. (left) King Hussein instituted this award in 1918 though formal issue of the medal most likely did not occur until late 1919. It was issued to commemorate the attack on Ma'an in April, 1918. In Arabic on the obverse of the medal: Ma'an 1337. The Hejira year of 1337 corresponds to October 7, 1918 to September 25, 1919, the time of issue for the medal. Independence Medal. (right) This medal commemorates the independence of the Hejaz as an independent Kingdom in 1916. On the obverse in Arabic "In commemoration of Independence 1334"

Second Class set of the Order of Al Nahda. The Second Class set consists of a breast star and badge. In the center are two crossed Hejaz flags. The gold disc states His Servant, Ali bin Al Hussein. The red enameled ring bears in Arabic, "Order of the Renaissance' and beneath that of the second class, 1334. The Hejira year 1334 corresponds to November 9, 1915 to October 27, 1916. The badge is suspended by woven cords. The Order was presented in a silk covered box with colors representing the Hejaz flag. Silver craftsmen in Mecca made most of the awards.

Second Class set of the Order of Istiqlal. The Second Class set consists of a breast star and badge. The red center in inscribed 'Al Hussein bin Ali. The Order of Istiqlal was awarded in five classes. The early Hejaz awards were suspended by woven cords of magenta, white and black. Later awards were suspended by a ribbon.

Order of Al Nahda Awards for service during the Arab Revolt.

Class of Award: **With Brilliants**

Allenby, Field Marshal Edmund Henry Hynman, Viscount Allenby, G.C.B., G.C.M.G. 8.3.1920

Class of Award: **First Class:**

MacMahon, Lieutenant-Colonel Sir Arthur Henry, G.C.M.G., G.C.V.O., K.C.I.E., C.S.I., retired Indian Army. 8.3.1920

Pelly, Rear-Adml. Henry B., C.B., M.V.O. 23.4.1920

Stack, Major (temporary Major-General) Sir Lee Oliver FitzMaurice, K.B.E., C.M.G., Border Regiment (Reserve of Officers). 8.3.1920

Vickery, Major and Brevet Lieutenant-Colonel (acting Lieutenant-Colonel) Charles Edwin, C.M.G., D.S.O., Royal Field Artillery. 18.8.1920

Wemyss of Wemyss, Adml. of the Flt. Baron Wester, G.C.B., C.M.G., M.V.O., D.C.L. 23.4.1920

Wilson, Major (temporary Lieutenant-Colonel) Cyril Edward, C.M.G., D.S.O., Retired Pay (Reserve of Officers). 24.10.1919

Wingate, General Sir Francis Reginald, G.C.B., G.C.V.O., G.B.E., K.C.M.G., D.S.O. 8.3.1920

Class of Award: **Second Class**

Bassett, Major (temporary Lieutenant-Colonel) John Retallack, D.S.O., O.B.E., Royal Bershire Regiment. 24.10.1919

Bols, Major-General Sir Louis Jean, K.C.B., K.C.M.G., D.S.O. 8.3.1920

Boyle, Capt. William H. D., C.B., Royal Navy. 23.4.1920

Campbell, Major-General Sir Walter, K.C.B., K.C.M.G., D.S.O. 8.3.1920

Clayton, Major and Brevet Lieutenant-Colonel (temporary Brigadier-General) Sir Gilbert Falkingham, K.C.B., C.B., C.M.G., Royal Garrison Artillery (Reserve of Officers). 8.3.1920

Cornwallis, Temporary Major (temporary Colonel) Kinahan, C.B.E., D.S.O., Special List. 8.3.1920

Cox, Major and Brevet Lieutenant-Colonel Charles Henry Fortnom, D.S.O., Royal Field Artillery. 16.1.1920

Dawnay, Captain and Brevet Major Alan Geoffrey Charles, C.B.E., D.S.O., Coldstream Guards. 8.3.1920

Fitzmaurice, Capt. Raymond, D.S.O., Royal Navy. 23.4.1920

Godwin, Brevet Colonel (temporary Brigadier-General) Charles Alexander Campbell, C.M.G., D.S.O., Indian Army. 9.4.1920

Groves, Air Commodore R. M., C.B., D.S.O., A.F.C.,
Al Qibla, 10,5, 1920

Joyce, Major and Brevet Lieutenant-Colonel Pierce Charles, C.B.E., D.S.O., Connaught Rangers. 8.3.1920

Lloyd, Captain Sir George Ambrose, G.C.I.E., D.S.O., Warwickshire Yeomanry. 8.3.1920

Newcombe, Major and Brevet Lieutenant-Colonel (temporary Lieutenant-Colonel) Stewart Francis, D.S.O., Royal Engineers. 16.1.1920

Pearson, Lieutenant-Colonel Hugh Drummond, D.S.O., Retired Pay, late Royal Engineers. 30.9.1920

Salmond, Air Vice-Marshal Sir William Geoffrey Hanson, K.C.M.G., C.B., D.S.O. (Royal Artillery). 1.4.1920

Stirling, Major (temporary Lieutenant-Colonel) Walter Francis, D.S.O., M.C., Royal Dublin Fusiliers (retired pay, Reserve of Officers). 8.3.1920

Taylor, Brevet Lieutenant-Colonel (temporary Colonel) Bertie Harry Waters, C.B.E., South Staffordshire Regiment. 9.4.1920

Wavell, Brevet Lieutenant-Colonel (temporary Brigadier-General) Archibald Percival, C.M.G., M.C., Royal Highlanders. 30.9.1920

Class of Award: **Third Class**

Bartholomew, Lieutenant-Colonel and Brevet Colonel (temporary Brigadier-General) William Henry, C.B., C.M.G., D.S.O., Royal Artillery. 8.3.1920

Batten, Captain William Douglas Grant, 3rd Gurkha Rifles, Indian Army. 19.8.1921

Borton, Group-Captain Amyas Eden, C.M.G., D.S.O., A.F.C., (Royal Highlanders). 1.4.1920

Cavendish, Lieut. Evan G. C., Royal Navy. 23.4.1920

Cookson, Christopher, Esq., M.B.E., Assistant Telegraph Engineer, Egyptian State Telephones, Cairo. 15.8.1922

Cunningham, Major and Brevet Lieutenant-Colonel (acting Lieutenant-Colonel) Aylmer Basil, C.B.E., D.S.O., Royal Engineers. 8.3.1920

Davenport, Major William Arthur, D.S.O., M.C., West Yorkshire Regiment. 16.1.1920

Davies, Lieutentant-Colonel and Brevet Colonel (temporary Brigadier-General) George Freshfield, C.B., C.M.G., C.B.E., Royal Army Service Corps. 8.3.1920

Garland, Temporary Captain Herbert, M.C., Special List. 16.1.1920

Garrod, Temporary 2nd Lieutenant (temporary Captain) Harry St. Clair, M.C., Special List. 16.1.1920

Gayer-Anderson, Major Robert Grenville, Royal Army Medical Corps. 6.2.1922

Goldie, Temporary Captain (Honorary Lieutenant in Army) Henry Mountford, Special List. 16.1.1920

Gottlieb, Temporary Lieutenant G. A. B., Royal Army Service Corps. 16.1.1920

Hindley, Captain Douglas Rowland, Indian Army (Reserve of Officers). 21.1.1921

Hobbs, Captain (temporary Major) Herbert Francis Clayton, The West Yorkshire Regiment. 21.1.1921

Hogarth, Cdr. David G., C.M.G., Royal Navy Volunteer Reserve. 22.1.1920

Hornby, Temporary Lieutenant (temporary Captain) Henry Sylvester, M.C., Royal Engineers. 8.3.1920

Linberry, Lieut.-Cdr. Thomas H., Royal Navy. 23.4.1920

McCheane, Lieutenant-Colonel (temporary Colonel) Montagu William Hiley, C.M.G., C.B.E., Royal Army Ordnance Corps. 8.3.1920

Mainwaring, Major Watkin Randle Kynaston, C.B.E., Denbighshire Yeomanry. 8.3.1920

Marshall, Captain and Brevet Major (acting Major) William Edward, M.C., M.B., Royal Army Medical Corps. 16.1.1920

O'Hara, Major and Brevet Lieutenant-Colonel (temporary Lieutenant-Colonel) Erril Robert, C.M.G., D.S.O., Royal Army Service Corps. 8.3.1920

Poignand, Cdr. Charles A., Royal Navy. 23.4.1920

Rashleigh, Cdr. Vernon S., Royal Navy. 8.6.1920

Snagge, Capt. Arthur I., Royal Navy. 22.3.1921

Symes, Major and Brevet Lieutenant-Colonel (temporary Lieutenant-Colonel) George Stewart, C.M.G., D.S.O., Hampshire Regiment. 8.3.1920

Turnbull, Major (temporary Lieutenant-Colonel) George Oliver, D.S.O., 26th Punjabs, Indian Army. 7.5.1920

Warren, Cmd. Arthur G., Royal Navy. 27.7.1920

Whitley, Captain Norman Pownall, M.C., 7th Battalion, Manchester Regiment (Territorial Force). 30.9.1920

Williams, Wing-Commander Richard, D.S.O., O.B.E. (Aust. Flying Corps). 1.4.1920

Winterton, Major Edward, Earl Winterton, T.D., Sussex Yeomanry (Territorial Force Reserve). 30.9.1920

Young, Captain Hubert Winthrop, D.S.O., 116th Mahrattas, Indian Army. 8.3.1920

Class of Award: **Fourth Class**

Baker, Major Dodington George Sherston, Indian Medical Service. 30.9.1920

Brackenbury, Local Captain G. H., employed Egyptian Expeditionary Force. 8.3.1920

Brodie, Temporary Lieutenant Samuel Henry, M.C., Royal Field Artillery. 8.3.1920

Clayton, Captain (temporary Major) Iltyd Nicholl, Royal Garrison Artillery. 8.3.1920

Clayton, Captain Norman Willis M.B.E., M.C., Machine Gun Corps, letter from Arab Bureau, 6.5.1920.

Dixon, Captain William, Bedfordshire and Hertfordshire Regiment. 30.9.1920

Dowsett, Temporary Lieutenant (acting Captain) Stanley Gordon, Machine Gun Corps. 8.3.1920

Feilding, Lieut. The Hon. Francis E. H. J., O.B.E., Royal Navy Volunteer Reserve. 22.1.1920

Fox, Temporary Lieutenant Horace George, Royal Army Service Corps. 30.9.1920

Furness-Williams, Squadron Leader Frederick William, M.C. 25.1.1921

Gilman, Temporary Lieutenant Leofric Hale, M.C., Machine Gun Corps. 8.3.1920

Goslett, Temporary Captain Raymond Gwynne, M.C., Royal Army Service Corps. 8.3.1920

Gray, Temporary Lieutenant William Lionel, General List. 30.9.1920

Greenhill, Temporary Leiutenant Edward Stanley, M.C., Machine Gun Corps. 30.9.1920

Grey, Temporary Captain Gerald Omar Rushie, Royal Army Medical Corps. 8.3.1920

Grisenthwaite, Temporary Lieutenant A. G., Machine Gun Corps. 30.9.1920

Hakim, Sub-Inspector Hakim Said, Police Officer attached to the British Agency at Jeddah. 9.5.1922

Hawley, Lieutenant Frederick Cecil, D.F.C., (Aust. Flying Corps). 1.4.1920

Henderson, Flt.-Lieut. Thomas, M.C., (R.E.). 1.4.1920

Higgins, Temporary Lieutenant (acting Captain) E. Scott, Royal Warwickshire Regiment. 8.3.1920

Hinde, Temporary Captain Arthur Reginald, Royal Army Service Corps. 30.9.1920

Holland, Temporary Captain Kenneth George, O.B.E., Royal Army Service Corps. 8.3.1920

Hopwood, Lieutenant Norman, 7th Battalion, Manchester Regiment (Territorial Force). 30.9.1920

James, Flight Lieut. H. Hindle, Al Qibla, 20.5.1920.

Kirkbride, Temporary Lieutenant Alec Seath, M.C., Labour Corps. 8.3.1920

Leith, Lieutenant Montagu Pemell, 4th Battation, Essex Regiment (Territorial Force). 30.9.1920

Littleton, Lieutenant (temporary Lieutenant-Colonel) The Honorable Charles Christopher Josceline, D.S.O., 7th Battalion, Middlesex Regiment (Territorial Force). 8.3.1920

McKibbin, Captain Frederick, M.B., Royal Army Medical Corps (Special Reserve). 30.9.1920

Mackintosh, Temporary Major Charles Alexander Gordon, Special List. 8.3.1920

Makins, F.O. (A./Flt.-Lt.) Arthur Dayer, D.F.C. 1.4.1920

Maynard, Major Percy Guy Wolfe, D.S.O., Royal Irish Rifles. 8.3.1920

Murphy, Lieutenant Arthur William, D.F.C. (Aust. Flying Corps). 1.4.1920

Nunan, Lieutenant Stanislaus Acton, (Aust. Flying Corps). 1.4.1920

Oldfield, Lieutenant Kenneth John, D.F.C. 25.1.1921

Pascoe, Temporary Lieutenant George Couldridge, Royal Field Artillery. 8.3.1920

Peake, Captain Frederick Gerald, West Riding Regiment. 8.3.1920

Perkins, Lieut.-Cdr. George T. W., Royal Navy. 27.7.1920

Peters, Lieutenant George Clifton, D.F.C. (Aust. Flying Corps). 1.4.1920

Powell, Local Lieutenant A., employed Egyptian Expeditionary Force. 8.3.1920

Pratt-Barlow, Captain and Brevet Major Edward A., King's Royal Rifle Corps (Reserve of Officers). 8.3.1920

Ramsey, Temporary Captain Graham Colville, M.B., Royal Army Medical Corps. 8.3.1920

Ryder, Temporary Captain Alfred Harold, General List. 8.3.1920

Salt, Lieut.-Cdr. Sir John W. T., Bt., Royal Navy. 27.7.1920

Scott, Temporary Major R. H., D.S.O., O.B.E., General List. 8.3.1920

Shah, Ressaidar Hasan, M.C., 9th Hodson's Horse, Indian Army. 8.3.1920

Siddons, Lieutenant Victor Donald, D.F.C. (Northts. Regt.). 1.4.1920

Smith, Captain Sir Ross, K.B.E., M.C., D.F.C., A.F.C. (Aust. Flying Corps). 1.4.1920

Spence, Temporary Lieutenant Hugh Gillies Cameron, Royal Army Service Corps. 30.9.1920

Stafford, Lieut. (now Flying Officer) William George, M.C., D.C.M. 2.9.1924

Stent, Squadron Leader Frederick William, M.C. 25.1.1921

Thomson, Lieut. (acting Captain) David Norris, M.C. 2.9.1924

Tookey, Temporary Lieutenant Harry Charles, Labour Corps. 30.9.1920

Wade, Temporary Lieutenant Ernest Henry, M.C., Machine Gun Corps. 30.9.1920

Walker, Temporary Lieutenant Thomas, Royal Army Service Corps. 30.9.1920

Ward, Lieut.-Cdr. Eric H., Royal Navy. 27.7.1920

Wordie, Major William, O.B.E., Royal Army Service Corps (Territorial Force). 8.3.1920

General Allenby and Emir Abdullah.
Allenby wears the Al Nahda "with brilliants" breast badge.

Colonel Stewart Newcombe
Newcombe in Royal Engineers full dress uniform wearing the
Second Class Order of Al Nahda.

Major W. E. Marshall
Major Marshall in Royal Army Medical Corps service dress
uniform wearing medals including the Military Cross with the
Third Class Order of Al Nahda around his neck.

Colonel Walter Francis Stirling
Colonel W. F. Stirling in Royal Dublin Fusiliers full dress uniform
with medals including the Second Class Order of Al Nahda.

Captain Hubert Winthrop Young
Captain Young in full dress civil uniform with medals including
the Third Class Order of Al Nahda.

Order of Al Nahda
Fourth Class Order of Al Nahda with presentation box awarded to
Major Percy Wolfe Maynard, Royal Irish Rifles.

T. E. Lawrence, London, 1919

Appendix 4
-Lawrence Photographs by Harry Chase-

Numbers and slide titles in **Bold** are from the original Lowell Thomas slide inventory at Marist College. The titles are by Lowell Thomas. Location of the photographic setting and where the photograph appears in print is in brackets. References: With Lawrence in Arabia. (WLA), Century, 1924. and Hutchinson, Tenth Edition. Some photographs have been cropped.

1.42 Col. Lawrence ¾ length.

(Hotel Fast, Jerusalem, 1918. WLA. Century, facing page 33. Asia, Sept. 1919, page 820. Worlds Work, July, 1921, page 281.)

1.43 Col. Lawrence, full length.

(Hotel Fast, Jerusalem, 1918. WLA. Century, facing page 8. Strand Magazine, January 1920, page 41.)

1.44 Col. Lawrence standing on prayer rug-Akaba.

(Akaba, 1918. Asia, December 1919, page 1206.)

1-45 T. E. Lawrence, D. G. Hogarth, Alan Dawnay.

a,b,c. (Cairo, 1918. Three versions, full length, half figure group shot and single standing figure of Lawrence. 1-45a, WLA. Century, facing page 241 with Dawnay cropped out. 1-45b, WLA, Century, facing page 33. Asia, December, 1919, page 1209.)

1.46 Lawrence on camel.

(Arabia, 1918. WLA. Hutchinson, facing page 41. This is not Lawrence. On a print at the Bodleian, labeled on the reverse by Lawrence; "Musafa Abdoula Akaba" with Abdoula crossed out. This photo appears in Asia, October 1919, page 1002, captioned "Two Members of Lawrence's Bodyguard.")

1.47 Lawrence and his bodyguard in desert.

(Arabia, 1918. WLA. Century, facing page 288 captioned "Sidi Lawrence and his sons." This group does not include Lawrence.)

1.48 Col. Lawrence and two Syrian advisors. (Feisal's house, Akaba, 1918. WLA. Century, facing page 189.)

1.49 Lawrence and British staff front of tent.

(Akaba, 1918. Strand Magazine, March 1920, page 261. Asia. April, 1920, page 266.)

1-50 Lawrence ¾ length – white, ends of headdress back over shoulders, hands clasped-VG.

(London, 1919. WLA. Century, facing page 96.)

1-51 Col. Lawrence in Paisley robe, squatting full face, close up, duplicate fine. (London, 1919.)

1-52 Col. Lawrence squatting, London, Paisley gown, V.G.

(London, 1919. WLA. Century, facing page 400. Asia, April 1920, page 256.)

1-53 Col. Lawrence in white sitting on floor, toe of boot showing.

(London, 1919. Boot has been scratched out.)

1-54 Col. Lawrence in white side view, three quarters, left hand on sword, fine.

(London, 1919. WLA. Century, facing page 404. Strand Magazine, March 1920, page 251.)

1-55 Col. Lawrence in white, three quarters front, hands behind back, headcloth over shoulders (London, 1919.)

1-56 Col. Lawrence in Paisley robe, three quarters both hands on sword, full face.

(London, 1919. WLA. Century, frontispiece. Strand Magazine, April, 1920, page 330.)

1-57 Col. Lawrence in white three quarters length full face, headcloth hanging down, fine.

(London, 1919. WLA, Century facing page 364.)

1-58 Col. Lawrence in white, three quarters side, hands clasped over knee. N.G.

(London, 1919. WLA. Hutchinson, facing page 133.)

1-58a Col. Lawrence in white, side view, sitting on floor, right hand on chin.

(London, 1919. WLA. Century, facing page 96.)

1-59 Col. Lawrence in white, three quarters, sitting on stool, not very good.

(London, 1919)

1-60 Col. Lawrence, Graphex, white robes, seated, side view.

(London, 1919.)

1-61 Col. Lawrence, Graphex, Paisley seated, side view, holding book.

(London, 1919. Strand Magazine, January, 1920, page 40.)

1-62 Col. Lawrence, full form, white robes. (London, 1919. Strand Magazine, February 1920, page 141. WLA. Hutchinson, facing page 280.)

1-63 Col. Lawrence, Graphex, sitting on rug, hand on each knee.

(London, 1919.)

1-68 Emir Feisal and cabinet in Akaba.

(Akaba, 1918. WLA. Century, facing page 304. Asia, September 1919, page 828.

No # Emir Feisal and cabinet in Akaba.

(Akaba, 1918.) Similar to 1-68 with Lawrence looking down.

1-72b Col. Lawrence and two Syrian advisors.

(Akaba, 1918. Enlarged copy of 1-48.)

4-2 Lowell Thomas and Col. Lawrence squatting before a tent, close up.

(Aba el Lissan, 1918. WLA. Century, facing page 177.)

4-3 Lowell Thomas and Col. Lawrence standing in front of tent.

(Aba el Lissan, 1918. WLA. Hutchinson, facing page 101.

4-4 Col. Lawrence and Lowell Thomas squatting in London, very good.

(London, 1919. Strand Magazine, March, 1920, page 257.)

4-5 Col. Lawrence and Mr. Thomas, three quarters, bushes, full face, best picture.

(London, 1919. World's Work, February 1927, page 365.)

4-6 Col. Lawrence and Mr. Thomas, side view, three quarters, bushes, serious, best picture. (London, 1919.)

4-7 Col. Lawrence and Mr. Thomas, squatting same as #12 and 82 only lighter for newspapers. (London, 1919, slightly different than 4-4.)

4-8 Col. Lawrence and Mr. Thomas, three quarters, with sickly smile.

(London, 1919.)

4-9 Col. Lawrence and Mr. Thomas, side view, laughing.

(London, 1919.)

4-15 Mr. Thomas and Col. Lawrence

(Aba el Lissan, 1918. Similar to 4-2 but Thomas and Lawrence looking at each other.)

2-178 Heavily veiled woman.

(Palestine, 1918. WLA. Century, facing page 357 with caption "Lawrence would occasionally disguise himself as a gipsy woman of Syria." This is not Lawrence.

1-42

1-43

1-44

1-45

1-46

1-47

1-48

1-49

1-50

1-51

1-52

1-53

1-54

1-55

1-56

1-57

1-58

1-58a

1-59

1-60

1-61

1-62

1-63

1-68

No#

1-72b

4-2

4-3

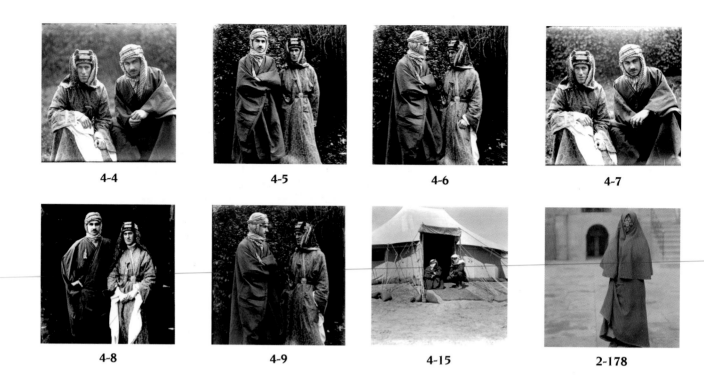

4-4 4-5 4-6 4-7

4-8 4-9 4-15 2-178

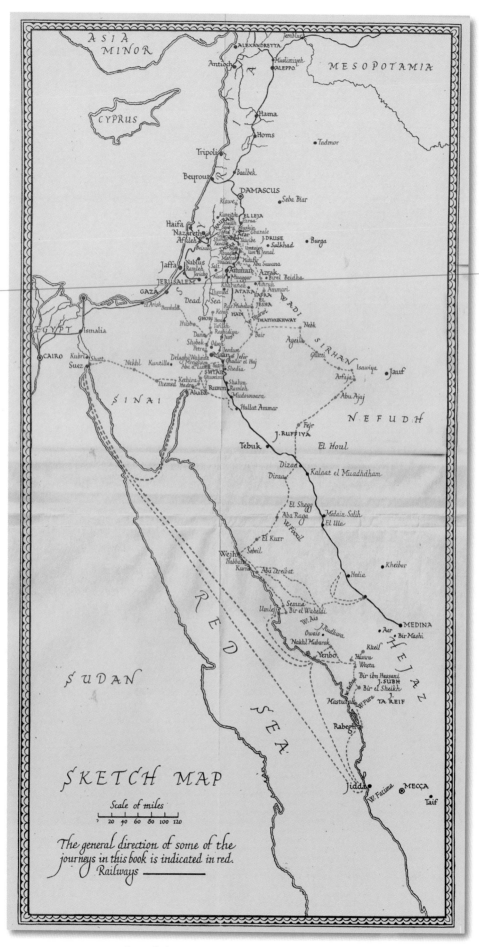

Map from the limited edition of Revolt in the Desert, 1927.

Appendix 5
-Maps-

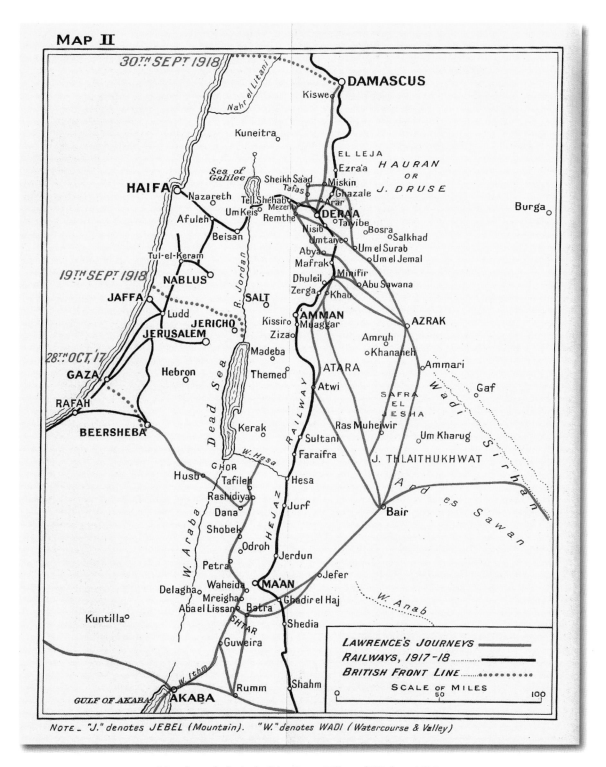

Map from the limited edition Seven Pillars of Wisdom, 1935.

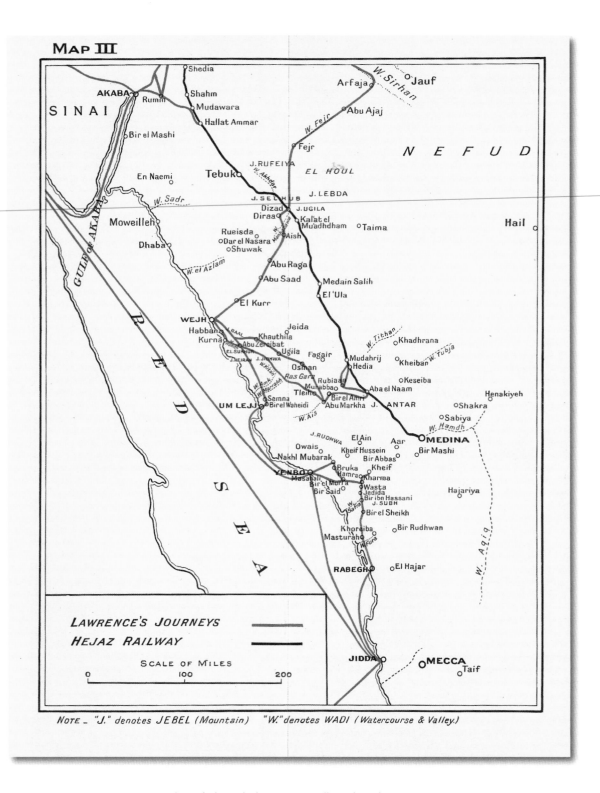

Map from the limited edition Seven Pillars of Wisdom, 1935.

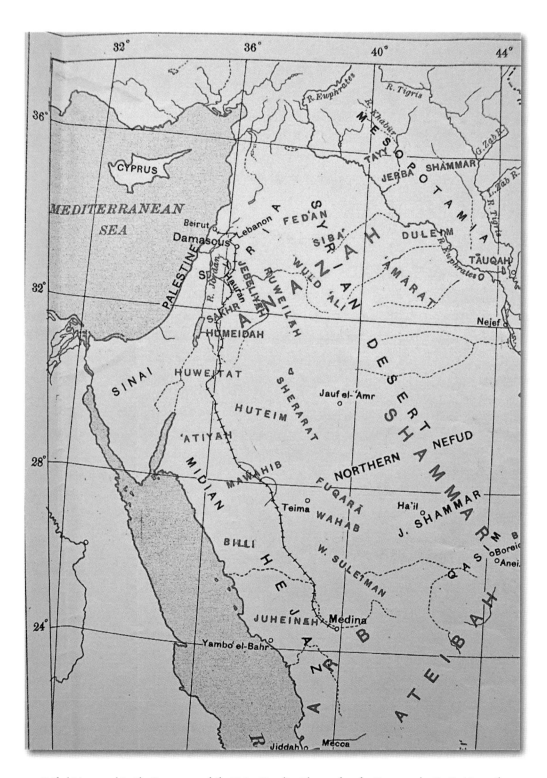

Tribal Map used in the Summary of the Hejaz Revolt with a preface by Commander D. G. Hogarth, prepared for the Arab Bureau.

-Acknowledgements-

Special thanks go to a number of people who have made this book possible. These include the gracious staff members of many libraries and institutions who have helped me in many different ways. I am especially grateful to Alan Jutzi and his staff at the Huntington Library, who so generously helped me with access to the Edwards Metcalf collection. Special thanks go to Colin Harris and his staff at the Bodleian Library, University of Oxford and to John Ansley, Director of the Archives, which include the Lowell Thomas papers at Marist College, who has been so supportive of my work. For their valuable assistance with the Lowell Thomas archives, my thanks also go to Claire Keith, Lowell Thomas Jr., and the late Fred Crawford.

I would also like to recognize the staffs of: the National Archives at Kew; the Liddell Hart Centre for Military Archives at King's College London; the Photograph Archive of the Imperial War Museum; and the Harry Ransom Humanities Research Center at Austin, Texas. I am most grateful to Michael Carey of the Seven Pillars of Wisdom Trust for allowing me to publish many of the wonderful Kennington pastels.

Many individuals offered their advice, shared their research and became friends along the way. Special thanks go to Jeremy Wilson, Detlef Hoffman, Roger Bragger, Ron Penhall, Pieter Shipster and Peter Laney, to Phil O'Brien, Charlie Eilers, Roland Schank, and Paul Helfer, to Shep Paine, Jim DeRogatis, Ron Leh, Lane and Anna Stewart and Mike Cobb.

I would also like to acknowledge the late Rory Moore of the Imperial Camel Corps for sharing with me his stories and sherry, and the late Edwards Metcalf, who was always willing to dig out more outstanding treasures for me to look at and study. And to Mena O'Connor, the daughter of Bimbashi Garland, now in her nineties, I give my thanks for her friendship, guidance and insights on life.

I extend special thanks to Carlos Andrea for understanding how I visualized this book and seeing it through. Thanks to Jose Garcinuño Martínez and Ricardo Recio Cardona for their diligence and attention to detail in every aspect of this book. Finally, I give a soft thank you to my wife, the noted author and art curator Gloria Groom, who finally gets her dining room table back, at least until the next book.

Major General Sir Granville Rylie lays a memorial wreath at the Imperial Camel Corps monument in London, 1930. Rylie was in command of the 2nd Light Horse Brigade. Earl Winterton, the tall figure on the left, looks on.

-Bibliography-

Lawrence's Writings:

Graves, R. and Liddell Hart, B., T. E. *Lawrence to his Biographers Robert Graves and Liddell Hart*, New York 1962

Lawrence, T. E., *Seven Pillars of Wisdom*, London 1935

Lawrence, T. E. and Woolley, L., *The Wilderness of Zin*, London 1936

The Letters of T. E. Lawrence, ed. Garnett, D., London 1938

The Home Letters of T. E. *Lawrence and His Brothers*, ed. Lawrence, M. R., Oxford 1954

Lawrence, T. E., *The Mint*, London 1955

Lawrence, T. E., *Crusader Castles*, Oxford 1988

The Letters of T. E. Lawrence, ed. Brown, M., New York 1989

Lawrence, T. E., *The Diary of* T. E. Lawrence 1911, Reading 1995

Lawrence, T. E., *Seven Pillars of Wisdom* (The Complete 1922 Oxford Text), Fordingbridge 2004

T. E. *Lawrence in War & Peace*, ed. Brown, M., London 2005

Biography:

Brown, M., *Lawrence of Arabia, the life, the legend*, London 2005

Brown, M. and Cave J., *A Touch of Genius*, New York 1989

Graves, R., *Lawrence and the Arabs*, London 1927

Graves, R. P., *Lawrence of Arabia and His World*, London 1976

Hyde, H., *Solitary in the Ranks, Lawrence of Arabia as Airman and Private Soldier*, New York 1978

Hoffman, D. and Fansa, M., ed. *Lawrence von Arabian Genese eines Mythos*, Oldenburg 2010

Lawrence, A. W., T. E. *Lawrence by His Friends*, London 1937

Liddell Hart, B., 'T. E. *Lawrence' in Arabia and After*, London 1934

Mack, J., A *Prince of our Disorder: The Life of* T. E. *Lawrence*, Boston 1976

Ocampo, V., 338171 T. E. (*Lawrence of Arabia*), New York 1963

Smith, C. Sydney, *The Golden Reign*, London 1940

Tabachnick S. and Matheson, C., *Images of Lawrence*, London 1988

Wilson, J., T. E. Lawrence, National Portrait Gallery Publications, London 1988.

Wilson, J., *Lawrence of Arabia, The Authorized Biography of* T. E. Lawrence, London 1989

Troops with Lawrence:
Officers:

Birdwood, Lord C. B., *Nuri As-Said*, London 1959

Facey, W. and Safwat, N., A *Soldier's Story, The Memoirs of Jafar Pasha Al-Askari*, London 2003

Jarvis, C. S., *Arab Command: the biography of Lieutenant-Colonel F. W. Peake Pasha*, London 1942

Kirkbride, A., *An Awakening*, University Press of Arabia 1971

Stirling, W. F., *Safety Last*, London 1953

Winterton, Earl, *Fifty Tumultuous Years*, London 1955

Young, H., *The Independent Arab*, London 1933

French in the Hejaz:

Bremond, E., *Le Hedjaz dans la Guerre Mondiale*, Paris 1931

Leclerc, C., *Avec* T. E. *Lawrence en Arabie, La Mission militarie francaise au Hedjaz 1916-1029*, Paris 1998

Leclerc, C., 'The French Soldiers in the Arab Revolt', *Journal of the* T. E. *Lawrence Society*, Vol. IX, No. 1, Autumn 1999

C Flight and X Flight:

Hynes, J., *Lawrence of Arabia's Secret Air Force*, Barnsley 2010

Knight, R., 'The Reverend Victor Donald Siddons, MBE, DFC, MA and the Siddons Collection', *The Journal of the* T. E. *Lawrence Society*, Vol. XVII, No. 1, Autumn 2007

Rudoe, B., *The Life and Times of Frank Thornton Birkinshaw*, London 2010

Seward, D., *Wings Over the Desert*, Yeovil 2009

West, J., 'Junor's Delivery', *The Journal of the* T. E. *Lawrence Society*, Vol. IX, No. 2, Spring 2000

Wright, P., with Bragger, R., 'Lawrence's Air Force', *Cross & Cockade International Journal*, Vol. 34, No 2, 2003

Imperial Camel Corps:

Berton, J., 'Lawrence and the Imperial Camel Corps', *The Journal of the* T. E. *Lawrence Society*, Vol. XX, No 2 (2010/11)

Inchbald, G., *Imperial Camel Corps*, London 1970

Langley, G. and E., *Sand, Sweat & Camels*, Kilmore 1976

The Royal Navy:

Cork and Orrey, Earl of, (Boyle, W.), *My Naval Life, 1886-1941*, London 1942

Parnell, C., 'Lawrence of Arabia's Debt to Seapower', *Procedings*, August 1979

Wemyss, Lady Wester, *The Life and Letters of Lord Wester Wemyss*, London 1935

Armoured Cars:

Armitage, H. St. J., and Pascoe, J., 'The 10 Pounder Motor Section R.F.A. Hedjaz Operations', *The Journal of the* T. E. *Lawrence Society*, Vol.X, No. 1, Autumn 2000

Pascoe, G., *'George C. Pascoe'*, *The Journal of the* T. E. *Lawrence Society*, Vol. IX, No. 1, Autumn 1999

Rolls, S. C., *Steel Chariots in the Desert*, London 1937

Stamps of the Hejaz:

Haworth, W. B. and Sargent, H. I., *The Postage Stamps of the Hejaz*, London 1922

Wilson, J., *The Hejaz, A History in Stamps*, State College 1982

Lowell Thomas, Harry Chase and the Travelogue:

Berton, J., 'The Harry Chase Photographs of T. E. Lawrence', *The Journal of the* T. E. *Lawrence Society*, Vol. XVII, No. 2, Spring 2008

Hodson, J., *Lawrence of Arabia and American Culture*, Westport 1995

Keith, C., 'The Lowell Thomas Papers'. *The Journal of the* T. E. *Lawrence Society*, Vol. VII, No. 2 (Spring 1998) and Vol. VIII, No. 2, Spring 1999

Thomas, L., *With Lawrence in Arabia*, New York, 1924

Arab Clothing:

Dickson, H., *The Arab of the Desert*, London 1949

Elgood, R., *The Arms and Armour of Arabia*, Aldershot 1994

Musil, A., *The Manners and Customs of the Rwala Bedouins*, New York 1928

Weir, Shelagh, *The Bedouin*, World of Islam Publishing Company 1976

Wilson, J., *T. E. Lawrence "Lawrence of Arabia"* Set of slides with a commentary, Oxford 1976

Ottoman Army:

Nicolle, D., *Ottoman Infantryman 1914-18*, Oxford 2010

Orses, T. and Ozcelik, N., *Turk Askeri Kiyafetleri*, Istanbul 2009

Motorcycles:

Knowles, R. *Two Superiors, the motor-cycling friendship of George Brough & T. E. Lawrence*, Upper Denby 2005

Payne, A., 'T. E. Lawrence and Brough Superior Motorcycles', *The Journal of the* T. E. *Lawrence Society*, Vol. XVIII, No. 2, 2008/9

Seven Pillars of Wisdom:

Thompson, V., *'Not a Suitable Hobby for an Airman'* – T. E. *Lawrence as Publisher and Writer*, Orchard Books 1986

Portraits of Lawrence:

Grosvenor, C., *An Iconography: The Portraits of* T. E. *Lawrence*, Pasadena 1988

Lawrence and the Movies:

Kelly, A., 'Lawrence Before Lean', *The Journal of the* T. E. *Lawrence Society*, Vol. IX, No. 1, Autumn 1999

Morris, L. and Raskin, L., *Lawrence of Arabia*, New York 1992

Silverman, S., *David Lean*, New York 1989

Turner, A., *The Making of David Lean's Lawrence of Arabia*, Limpsfield 1994

Lawrence as Photographer:

Lawrence, A. W., ed., *Oriental Assembly*, London 1939

The Hejaz Railway:

Usul, I. ed. *The Hejaz Railway, Album of Photographs*, Istanbul 1999

Nicholson, J., *The Hejaz Railway*, London 2005

Tourret, R., *Hedjaz Railway*, Abington 1989

Collecting Lawrence:

Christie's, *Printed Books and Manuscripts, December 7 1990*. New York 1990 (including the Lawrence collection of Bruce Tovee)

Christie's, *The Spiro Family Collection, Part II, 26 February 2004*, New York 2004 (including the Lawrence collection of the Spiro family)

Maggs Bros. Ltd. *Catalogue 1055 T. E. Lawrence*, London

O'Brien, P., *T. E. Lawrence: A Bibliography*, New Castle 2000

O'Brien, P., 'The Building of the Edwards H. Metcalf Collection of T. E. Lawrence Material', *The Journal of the* T. E. *Lawrence Society*, Vol. XIX, No. 1, 2009/10

Sotheby's, *Fine Books and Manuscripts, December 11, 12, 1984*, New York 1984 (including the Lawrence collection of Robert Payne)

Hejaz Orders and Medals:

Raw-Rees, O., 'The Orders and Medals of the Kingdom of the Hijaz', *The Journal of the Orders and Medals Society of America*, May-June 2001

Raw-Rees, O., 'The Order of Al Nahda of the Kingdom of the Hijaz', *The Journal of the Orders and Medals Research Society*, March 2003

Raw-Rees, O., 'Feisal's Arab Army: The British Awards', *The Journal of the Orders and Medals Research Society*, March 2006

Lawrence bust by Derwent Wood, 1919.

-Photo Sources and Credits-

In the following listed sources the James A. Cannavino Library, Archives and Special Collections, Marist College, USA is represented as Marist College, the Imperial War Museum, London, is represented as IMW and The Edwards Metcalf Collection of the Huntington Library is represented as Metcalf Collection.

Front cover, spine, back cover, front flap) Marist College

Page 4) Marist College

Page 5) IWM Q 10212

Page 6) Marist College

Page 8) IWM UNI 12240

Page 9) IWM

Page 10) Bodleian Library, Ms. Photogr.c.122,f.1

Page 11 top) Bodleian Library, Ms.Photogr.c.126,f.3r

Page 11 bottom) Bodleian Library, Ms.Eng.c.6742,f.44

Page 12 top) Berton

Page 12, bottom) Bodleian Library, Ms.Photogr.c.122,f.3

Page 13) Berton

Page 14, top left) Jesus College, Oxford

Page 14) *Crusader Castles*, Golden Cockerel Press.

Page 15 top) Berton

Page 15 Private Collection

Page 16) British Museum

Page 17) British Museum

Page 18) British Museum

Page 19) British Museum

Page 20) Berton

Page 22-23) *Palestine Exploration Fund Annual*, 1914-1915

Page 24) Berton

Page 26 top) *Sir Archibald Murray's Despatches*, London, 1920.

Page 26 bottom.) Marist College

Page 27 top) Berton

Page 27 bottom) IWM Q 59375

Page 28) IWM Q 59956

Page 29) *Lawrence and the Arabs* by Graves

Page 30) Illustrated London News

Page 31 left) Australian War Memorial REL AWM 16513

Page 32 right) Garst Museum, Greenville, Ohio

Page 33) Marist College.

Page 33 top) Berton

Page 34) Berton

Page 35) Private collection

Page 36) IWM Q 58860

Page 37) IWM Q 58861

Page 38 Library of Congress

Page 39 IWM Q 59086

Page 40) IWM Q 59110

Page 41) IWM Q 59326

Page 42) IWM Q 59084

Page 43) IWM Q 59000

Page 44 top) Tank Museum

Page 44 bottom) Sotheby's London, Important Costumes, 7 Nov. 96, lot 143

Page 45 Berton

Page 46 top left) Berton

Page 46, top right) Berton

Page 47 top) Private Collection

Page 47 bottom) Bodleian Library, Ms.Photogr.c.124,f.65

Page 48) Private

Page 49) IWM Q 59556

Page 50 top) National Archives, Kew

Page 50 bottom) National Archives, Kew

Page 51 top) *Lawrence and the Arabs* by Graves

Page 51 bottom) Berton

Page 52) IWM, Q 59587

Page 53) Metcalf Collection

Page 54 top) Berton

Page 55) Marist College

Page 56) Metcalf Collection

Page 56-7) Marist College

Page 58 top) Metcalf Collection

Page 58-59) Marist College

Page 59 top) Marist College

Page 60) Roger Bragger

Page 61,top, bottom) Roger Bragger

Page 62, top) Metcalf Collection

Page 62, bottom) Metcalf Collection

Page 63) IWM Q 60059

Page 64 top left) IWM Q 59873

Page 64, top right) Berton

Page 64, bottom) Metcalf Collection

Page 65 top) IWM Q 58703

Page 65 bottom) IWM ART 3198

Page 66) IWM Q 59091

Page 67) Ministere de la Culture, Mediatheque de l'architecture et du patrimoine.

Page 67, middle right) Berton

Page 68) Marist College

Page 69) Bodleian Library, Ms.Photogr.c.123/2,f.181

Page 70 top) Private Collection

Page 70, bottom) Berton

Page 71 top) IWM Q 59352

Page 72 bottom) Bodleian Library Ms.Photogr. c.123/1,f.47

Page 72 top) IWM Q 59338

Page 72, bottom) National Archive, Kew

Page 73) Mena O'Connor

Page 74 top) *Arab Command* by C. S. Jarvis

Page 74, bottom) Berton

Page 75 top) Berton

Page 75, bottom) Bodleian Library, Ms.Photogr.c.123/1,f.304

Page 76, top) Marist College

Page 76, bottom) Berton

Page 77) *Safety Last* by Col. W. F. Stirling

Page 78 top) IWM Q 58908

Page 78 bottom) DNW auction catalogue, 29 July, 1992

Page 79 top) Marist College

Page 79 bottom) Berton

Page 80) Private Collection

Page 81 top) Metcalf Collection

Page 81 bottom) Private Collection

Page 82 middle left) Sydney Smith's copy of Graves biography

Page 82 middle right) Metcalf Collection

Page 82 bottom) Berton

Page 83 top) Metcalf Collection

Page 83 middle) *Lawrence and the Arabs* by Graves

Page 83, bottom left) Christie's London. Exploration and Travel, 17 September, 1999, Lot 19.

Page 84 top) *The Life and Letters of Lord Wester Wemyss* by Lady Wemyss

Page 84 bottom) from *My Naval Life 1886-1941* by Admiral of the Fleet the Earl of Cork and Orrery

Page 85 top) IWM Q38828

Page 85 bottom) IWM SP 2072

Page 86 top left) Barbara Rudoe

Page 86 top right) *The Times History of the War*, Part 112.

Page 86 middle) *My Naval Life*.

Page 86 bottom) Marist College.

Page 87 top) Marist College

Page 87 bottom) Lawrence and the Arabs by Graves

Page 88) Berton

Page 89) Private collection

Page 90) Berton

Page 91) Berton

Page 92) Marist College

Page 93) Sydney Smith's copy of Graves biography

Page 94 top) *Generals of the Army* by Francis Dodd

Page 94 bottom) Private collection

Page 95 top) Berton

Page 95 bottom) Sydney Smith's copy of Graves biography

Page 96 top) Ministere de la Culture, Mediatheque de l'architecture et du patrimoine

Page 96 bottom) Marist College

Page 97 top) Metcalf Collection

Page 97 bottom) Marist College

Page 98-99) Marist Collection

Page 100 top left) Private Collection

Page 100 top right) IWM Q60062

Page 100 bottom) Bodleian Library, Ms.Photor.125/2,f.227

Page 101 top) Berton

Page 101 bottom) IWM Q 103773

Page 102) Berton photo, All Souls College, Oxford

Page 103) IWM FIR 8255

Page 104 top) British Library, London

Page 104 bottom) Private collection

Page 105 top) IWM Q 60099

Page 105 bottom) Berton

Page 106 top left) Australian War Memorial, REL AWM 17222

Page 106 top right) Berton

Page 106 middle) Sotheby's London, Important Costumes, 7 November 1996, Lot 143

Page 106 bottom left) Sotheby's London, 2 November 1995, Lot 186

Page 107 top left) Imperial War Museum

Page 107 top right) Ashmolean Museum, Oxford EA1965.176

Page 107 bottom) Berton

Page 108 top) Marist College

Page 108 bottom left) IWM Q 60101

Page 108 bottom right) IWM Q59174

Page 109 top left) IWM Q 60214

Page 109 top right) Australian War Memorial, BO2170

Page 109 bottom) Marist College

Page 110) IWM Q 58807

Page 111) Bodleian Library

Page 112) IWM Q58837

Page 191) Private Collection

Page 192-3) Private Collection

Page 194) Private collection

Page 195) Berton

Page 196 top) IMW OMD 419

Page 196 Bottom) Berton

Page 197 left) Oriental Institute, University of Chicago

Page 197 right) Berton

Page 198) Berton

Page 200 left) Private collection

Page 200 right) DNW auction catalogue, 29 July, 1992

Page 201 top left) Marist College

Page 201 top right) *Safety* Last by Col. W. F. Stirling

Page 201 bottom left) Martin Young

Page 201 bottom right) Berton

Page 202) Marist College

Page 204-7) Marist College

Page 208-9-10) Seven Pillars of Wisdom Trust

Page 211) The National Archives, Kew

Page 213) Berton

Page 216) IWM Art 4429